The Ladies of Monmouth

The Baptist Ladies' Cook Book

Choice and Tested Recipies

The Ladies of Monmouth

The Baptist Ladies' Cook Book
Choice and Tested Recipies

ISBN/EAN: 9783744781855

Printed in Europe, USA, Canada, Australia, Japan

Cover: Foto ©Lupo / pixelio.de

More available books at **www.hansebooks.com**

Peoples' National Bank,

of Monmouth, Illinois.

Capital $75,000.00.   Surplus $20,000.00.

A General Banking Business Transacted.

OFFICERS

WM. S. WEIR, President.   GEO. E. ARMSBY, 2d Vice-Pres.
WM. B. SMITH, Vice-Pres.   H. B. SMITH, Cashier.
E. D. BRADY, Teller.

We Don't Look for Much

From you—Mothers, Wives and Sweethearts—but please use your influence with the "boys" to

Have Their Clothes Made,

ot glued together.   "Send 'em to us."

WRIGHT & GRAHAM,

ARTISTIC TAILORS.

THE

...PTIST LADIES'

BOO...

Ask your Grocer for "Fidelity Brand." For sale at all first-class grocers.

For All Things Necessary

To good housekeeping in Dry Goods, Notions, Etc.,

Call at Montgomery's,

Always on hand, the very best assorted lines of Dress Goods, Hosiery and Underwear, Linens and Fancy Articles.

Every Department

Kept full and complete.

N. W. Montgomery & Co.

QUINBY BLOCK.

"... ers, wives and sisters of ...
teract ... oholics, by supplying plenty of ...
enjoya... "

PREFACE.

"Things for the cook, sir;
... I know not what."—*Romeo and Jul...*

In ...ng this Book of Recipes to ...
we des... ay that it has not been the ...
the co...ee to give a complete cook ...
in all ...ments.

But ... trust it will prove an assistan...
the ho...epers who are engaged in the stup...
ous ta... cooking for the nation.

Our ... thanks are extended to the ladies of ...
Monmo... for the recipes. The signatures are a
sufficient guarantee for their excellence.

We especially ask our friends to read the advertisements that they may know who have given us substantial aid. We ask for them an increased patronage, which their generosity to all our public enterprises justly merits.

COMPILERS.

National Bank of Monmouth

CAPITAL STOCK PAID UP, $100,000.00.
SURPLUS, $165,000.00.

HENRY TUBBS, President.   W. B. YOUNG, Cashier;
JNO. SPROUT, Vice-Pres.   JAS. FRENCH, Ass. Cash.

DIRECTORS—

Henry Tubbs,	Wm K. Stewart,	Jas. Firoved,
Wm. C. Norcross,	Ivory Quinby,	John Sprout,
O. S. French,	Geo. E. Miller,	W. Harrison Frantz,
Wm. Firoved,		Hiram Sheldon.

Transacts a General Banking Business in all its Departments; also,

Money to Loan on any time desired, at Lowest Rate and on Easiest Terms.

WEIR PLOW CO.,

MANUFACTURERS OF

Plows, Cultivators, Harrows,

Corn Planters,

Cotton Planters, Listers,

Rakes, and

Other Farm Machinery.

MONMOUTH, ... ILLINOIS.

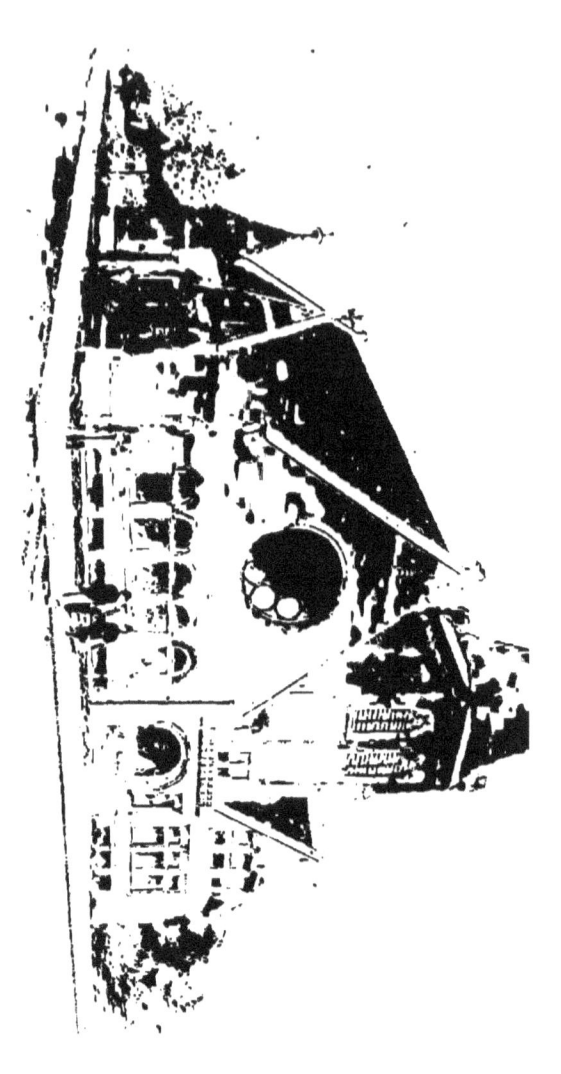

......THE......

Warren Co. Library

......CONTAINS THE......

Best Books and Periodicals

In all departments of Literature and Science, also on Housekeeping, Cookery, Sewing, Fancy Work, Home Decoration, Current Fashions, Health, Home Building, Gardening and all practical matters.

The best books for the young are carefully selected. 16,000 volumes are now on the shelves and 600 more new books are bought each year. New, fresh magazines are loaned out as soon as published, such as Harper's, The Century, The Atlantic, Cosmopolitan, The Bazar, Demorest, Delineator, North American Review, Review of Reviews, Ladies' Home Journal, Art Interchange, Art Amateur, and many others.

Three Dollars per year gives the use at home of these Books and Periodicals.

All persons are invited to read them at any time without charge in the Free Reading Room.

SOUPS.

"Expect spoon meat."—*Comedy of Errors.*

"The pot must smile but never laugh."

In making soups, put all uncooked meats and bones in cold water. If cooked in hot water, adding a little at a time. Use a flat-bottomed pot and keep on top of stove. It is better if made the day before wanted. When cold remove fat, re-heat and strain, adding vegetables as desired. Brown stock is made of beef shins and a piece of coarse beef. White stock, of veal shins and an old fowl, if you choose. One shin of veal will make three quarts of good veal stock, one hind shin of beef will make five quarts—a piece of each makes the best soup. All kinds of bones can be used, and all liquor in which beef, mutton or poultry is boiled. Wash shins—put on in cold water, skim just before it boils, simmer slowly four or five hours or longer. Boil vegetables separately, and add to soup stock a short time before serving. Barley, rice, tapioca, vermicelli, maccaroni and all vegetables may be used separately or together. Also, add the water in which they are boiled. Serve very hot.

To make rice. vermicelli, maccaroni or barley soup, boil thoroughly in separate vessel and add about quarter of an hour before serving. Cabbage, tomatoes or the soup boquet, or other vegetables may be also added, separately or together.

Hodgens' Ice Cream.

SOUPS.

BOUILLON.

Four pounds juicy beef, one tablespoon salt, two pounds bone, one tablespoon mixed herbs, four peppercorns, four cloves, two quarts water. Cut meat and bones in small pieces, boil down to three pints, season to taste. Add one onion, one-half carrot and turnip if you like; strain and re-heat.

ASPARAGUS SOUP.
S.

One bunch of asparagus boiled in a quart of salted water for twenty minutes. Press the asparagus through a colander. Put a quart of milk into a double boiler, adding a little parsley and a piece of onion. For thickening use two ounces of butter and three level tablespoonsfuls of flour rubbed together and thinned by stirring in a little of the milk. Then stir into the boiling milk and stir continually until it thickens. Have the asparagus and water in which it was cooked, hot and mix all together. Season and serve at once.
S.

CELERY SOUP.
S. C. K.

Take four or six stalks of celery, wash and cut into small pieces, using the leaves as well, cover with a pint or more of boiling water, and let boil half an hour. Press through a colander, do not drain, but allow the water to go through with the celery. Have in a double boiler one quart of *boiling milk* and a slice of onion, to this add the celery and water. Rub together one tablespoon of butter and two tablespoons of flour. Stir into boiling soup. Season with pepper and salt, and serve.

C. Shultz for anything in the Drug line.

CELERY SOUP.—NO. 2.

Take the white part of two large heads of celery. Either grate or chop fine, set to boil with a cup of rice, in water enough to cover. Allow the rice and celery to slowly stew until they can be rubbed through a coarse seive. Have hot one pint of milk and an equal quantity of strong chicken or veal broth. Pepper and salt to taste,

NOODLE SOUP.

Amanda Reichard.

One egg, two tablespoonsful of water, a little salt, add to this flour to make it just as stiff as possible, mixing all well together. Roll very thin, and with a cloth under allow it to remain on the board about two hours to dry, then fold in a roll and with a sharp knife cut very fine, drop it slowly, stirring lightly, into two quarts of boiling stock of chicken or beef, the former oftener used. Boil briskly ten minutes, keeping the pot tightly covered.

CHICKEN SOUP.

To one chicken put five pints of cold water and a slice of fat bacon, and boil it down to a quart. Just before taking from fire, add a cup of cream and a little thyme or parsley to season. Thicken as usual—one tablespoonful of flour, rubbed into one tablespoonful of butter.

Barley and rice are both nice for chicken soup. They should be boiled slowly, in a separate vessel and added to the soup about half an hour before removing from the fire.

John C. Dunbar, Druggist, Monmouth, Ill.

SOUPS.

NOODLES FOR SOUP.

Beat one egg very light, add a pinch of salt and flour enough to make a thick dough. Roll out into a thin sheet, dredge with flour to keep from sticking, then roll up lightly. Begin at one end and shave fine, as for slaw. Nice used in chicken soup.

CONSOMME.

One and one-half pounds of lean beef, same of lean veal, cut veal and one-half the beef in half inch cubes, remove all fat and put two quarts of cold water. Let the water simmer slowly, and take the remaining three-fourths pound of beef and cut into cubes, and brown in a tablespoonful of butter. Add browned meat to the other mixture to give the stock color, and let it simmer four or five hours. Take one-fourth cup each of carrot, onion and celery, when the soup has cooked four hours, put them in a pan with one tablespoonful of butter, and cook five minutes. Add to soup. Add also, one tablespoonful of salt, six peppercorns, three cloves, three allspice berries, one-half bay leaf, a sprig each of summer savory, marjoram, parsley and thyme, and cook one hour longer. Strain and cool, use to clear the white of one egg and shell, to each quart of stock.

OYSTER SOUP.

Mrs. John Gettemy.

One quart oysters, three pints milk brought to boil, in which stir one-half cup of finely powdered crackers, butter size of egg, pepper and salt to taste. Last add oysters and bring to boil. Serve hot.

New and lovely Japanese Napkins at McQuiston's.

FRENCH GUMBO SOUP.
E. P. Phelps, Atlantic, Iowa.

Three slices of bacon, three onions, one young, tender chicken, one quart tender okra pods, three green peppers. Fry the bacon to a light brown, cut up the onions and put in the bacon fat and let them fry. Cut the chicken in small pieces and fry with the bacon fat and onions to a light brown. Add the peppers cut fine, and the okra cut in small pieces. Pour over the whole two quarts of boiling water. Cook till tender and season to taste.

GREEN CORN SOUP.
Amanda Reichard.

Half a dozen ears of sweet corn; cut it off of the cob very fine, and put it in three pints or two quarts of boiling water, with one teaspoon of salt, two tablespoons of butter, and one-half teacup of sweet cream or new milk. Beat one egg with two tablespoons of sifted flour, mixed with sweet milk or water sufficiently thin to drop through a perforated ladle. Stir it lightly into the soup after it has boiled ten or fifteen minutes, then boil all together about three minutes, having the pot tightly covered all the time.

CREAM OF OYSTER SOUP.
Amy R. Rogers.

Boil one quart milk with one tablespoon of flour wet with milk five minutes, stirring all the time to prevent burning. Add one-half teaspoon-salt and one-half saltspoon white pepper and the liquor from one can oysters. Cook five minutes longer, add a tablespoonful of butter and strain before serving.

"ROLLING-PIN" CLEANED CURRANTS ARE READY FOR INSTANT USE. NO WASHING OR CLEANING REQUIRED.

CORN SOUP.

Grate, or slit the grains and scrape six ears of sweet corn. Boil cobs in one pint or more of water twenty minutes. Remove cobs and put in corn and boil fifteen minutes; then add one quart of rich milk. Season with salt, pepper and butter. Boil the whole ten minutes and turn into a tureen in which the yolks of three eggs have been well beaten. If a thick soup is desired, use one tablespoonful of flour rubbed into the butter.

DUCHESS SOUP.

Two slices each of carrot and onion cooked in one tablespoon of butter five minutes. Add one quart of white stock, either veal or chicken, one small blade of mace. Cook fifteen minutes. Melt two tablespoon butter, stir in two tablespoons of flour until free from lumps. Add gradually seasoned stock, also one tablespoon of salt, one saucespoon of pepper, mixed together, and one pint of milk or thin cream; stir in four rounding tablespoons of grated cheese; cook two minutes, serve.

POTATO SOUP.
Mrs. Geo. G. Wallace, Omaha.

A cheap, savory and warming soup. Take four good-sized potatoes, pare and slice thin. Also, an onion sliced thin and boiled with potatoes in enough water to keep from drying, until potatoes are ready to fall to pieces. Stir in a pint of milk, a tablespoonful of flour, a generous lump of butter, salt and pepper. Serve steaming hot.

Why don't you buy your Candies at the Bell Candy Kitchen, where they are all home made and fresh. D. Wilson, proprietor, Monmouth, Ill.

POTATO SOUP.

One quart of milk, six potatoes, one stalk of celery, slice of onion, and sprig of parsley. Boil milk, celery, onion and parsley together. Boil potatoes till tender, then mash. Add the boiling milk gradually to the potatoes, and press through a strainer. Season with salt, pepper and tablespoonful butter. Do not boil after the potatoes and milk are mixed. To keep warm, place over boiling water.

MEATLESS TOMATO SOUP.
Emma Gregg, Margaret Dunbar, Mrs. Geo. Babcock.

One quart tomatoes, one quart water. Stew till soft. Add one teaspoonful soda and allow to effervesce. Heat one quart new milk, add pepper, salt, butter and rolled crackers, strain tomatoes and add to milk.

MUSHROOM SOUP.
Mrs. Louie Babcock Tabor, Denver.

Milk three pints, one can mushrooms, one teaspoon salt, one saltspoon pepper, one tablespoon butter, yolks of three eggs. Put the milk on in double boiler and let boil, then add mushrooms, chopped fine; also, the liquor which is over them. Then put in the seasoning, and last, the eggs, well beaten.

TOMATO SOUP.
Mrs. Wildemuth.

One can of tomatoes, one pint water, add four cloves, one onion, and one teaspoonful corn starch, browned in butter. Put together and strain through colander. Cook one-half hour. Salt and pepper to taste.

Hodgens, Fine Candy.

PEA SOUP.

Mrs. W. B. Jenks, Chicago.

Half peck young green peas. Shell and boil peas and pods separately. Mash peas and strain through colander. Strain water off pods and mix with peas. Just before serving add one quart of rich milk, or part cream, butter size of egg and salt.

PURIE OF CLAMS.

Mrs. Overton, Boston.

Two cans or one quart of fresh clams, add one quart of white stock. Simmer one hour if raw, and fifteen minutes if canned clams are used. Rub clams through a sieve until only the hard parts remain. Add one-half onion fried in two tablespoon of butter and flour. Pour on clam liquor and add one teaspoon of salt, one saucespoon of pepper, a sprig of parsley and a bit of mace. Cook ten minutes and dilute with one quart of milk. Beat the yolks of four eggs, and add to soup slowly so as to avoid coagulation, serve.

CRISPED CRACKERS.

To serve with soup, split butter or use wafer crackers. Spread lightly with butter, brown quickly in hot oven.

The finest Cream Tartar and Baking Soda, at Dunbar's Drug Store.

The Vienna Bread

Has no equal. Everybody says so. Try it and you won't care to bother with these recipes.

Rye and Graham Bread, Rolls, Fine Cakes, Doughnuts. Cookies, etc., etc. always on hand.

We use the Best Materials.

GIBSON & MILLER.
MAIN ST.

G. S. BARNES,

THE DRUGGIST,

Carries a full and complete line of Drugs, Medicines and Druggists' Sundries, Books, Stationery and Fancy Goods, Spices and Extracts. Cold Soda Water in summer and hot in winter. All the Novelties in their season.

Postoffice Block.   G. S. BARNES.

PILLSBURY & SAWYER,
—DEALERS IN—

Hardware, Cultery, Stoves, Tinware, Farm Implements, Wagons, Buggies, Harness, Rubber and Leather Belting, Wind Mills, Pumps etc.

North Side Square, - - - **Monmouth, Ill.**

G. W. CUTLER,

GROCER.

Has always selected Fruits and Vegetables in season. Also Fresh country Butter and Eggs

South Main Street.

WM. H. RANKIN,
FURNITURE,

SOUTH MAIN STREET.

W. W. McCULLOUGH & CO.,
LUMBER,
Hard and Soft Coal and Wood,

MONMOUTH, ILLINOIS.

Are you thinking of buying a new Stove or Range—one that will burn the least fuel, cause the least trouble, give the greatest degree of heat, last the longest and look the best? Then **Jewel Stoves and Ranges** will interest you.

For efficiency, economy, durability, and beauty, they represent the zenith of the stovemaker's skill. Ask to see them at the dealers. Look for the above trade mark.

PINKERTON & EVANS, Southeast Cor. Square

FISH.

"This fish was well fished for."—*Winter's Tale.*

FISH A LA CREME.

Mrs. Draper Babcook.

One pound of salmon, cod or haddock, one and one-half cups of milk, one cup of crackers, rolled; one tablespoonful of butter, one tablespoonful of flour, one saltspoonful of salt and pepper. Spread the boiled fish on a platter, put the butter in a pan on the stove with the salt and pepper. When it boils up add the flour, have the milk hot and put in slowly, stirring all the time, turn this over the boiled fish. Moisten the crackers in butter and put over the top, put in the oven over a tin dish of water, brown, then take one cup of hot mashed potatoes and put through the sieve around the edge. Serve hot.

ESCALLOPED FISH.

Mrs. J. D. Diffenbaugh.

Boil three pounds of fish until tender, take out the bone. Dressing—one quart milk, salt, pepper, one tablespoonful butter and three tablespoonfuls of corn starch. Boil to a thick dressing; line the platter with a layer of dressing, then of fish, etc., etc., the last being the dressing; sprinkle over top bread or cracker crumbs. Bake one-half hour and serve on the same platter.

C. Shultz' Drug and Fine Perfumery

CREAMED SALMON.
Mrs. E. J. Pillsbury.

Drain all the liquid from a can of salmon and chop the salmon fine ; grease the bottom of a small baking dish and put in a layer of bread crumbs, then a layer of fish and so on until you have used a pint of crumbs and the fish. Dressing—Boil a pint of milk, add two tablespoonfuls of butter, and salt and pepper to taste ; pour this over the salmon and bread crumbs, and bake until brown. Have the top layer bread crumbs.

BAKED WHITEFISH.

Cleanse carefully. Wipe dry, rub with salt and dredge with flour, fill with dressing, and tie up or sew. Place in hot pan with a few slices of salt pork across it, or use butter. Pour in enough hot water to prevent burning. A four or five pound fish will require from one to one and a half hours. If a cloth is put in the pan first, the fish can be lifted up without breaking. Dressing :—Use bits of stale bread soaked in cold water, press dry, add one onion chopped fine, salt, pepper and butter. Add two or three eggs if desired.

CODFISH BALLS.
S. B.

Pick three-fourths of a pound of codfish very fine. Wash in several waters or soak fifteen minutes. Boil with a dozen medium sized potatoes—putting the codfish on top. When tender drain and make very fine, add two beaten eggs, butter the size of an egg, pepper to taste. Make into cakes, dip in beaten eggs. Roll in cracker crumbs and fry in boiling lard.

The correct thing in Invitation and Menu Cards, always at McQuiston's.

CREAM FISH.

Mrs. Eliza B. Smith.

Two pounds of white fish or red snapper. Boil it after the fish has been skinned and boned, pick it into fine pieces; one-half cup butter and two-thirds pint or more of cream. Put the cream on the stove in a double boiler. Put two tablespoon- of flour into the butter, add pepper and salt to taste, and put into the boiling cream. Beat until done. Pour this over the fish. Mix thoroughly with the grated rind and about half of the juice of a lemon. Put into the baking dish and cover with cracker crumbs. Dampen by pouring one table-spoonful of melted butter. Then bake and serve hot. Will serve ten persons.

CODFISH STEW.

K. C.

Shred the fish and let it soak in cold water to freshen. When ready to cook pour on boiling water and let it stand a few minutes, then drain and pour on fresh boiling milk. Allow one quart of milk to one cup of fish. Season with salt, pepper and butter, and thicken with a little flour. If desired add one or two eggs, well beaten or broken in whole and lightly stirred in, or the eggs may be previously boiled. K. C.

BAKED CODFISH.

Pick up one teacup of codfish, Let it cook in lukewarm water while you mix two cups of cold mashed potatoes with one pint of sweet milk, two eggs, a good sized lump of butter, pepper and salt if necessary. Add codfish. Mix all together. Pour in pudding dish and bake twenty-five or thirty minutes.

Hodgens' Confectionery.

BOILED SALMON OR HALIBUT.

Mrs. A. B. Seaman,

Three or four pounds of fish. Dip in boiling water and scrape clean. Rub with salt and pepper. Put in pan and pour milk over it till half an inch deep. Bake about an hour, basting with the milk. The milk keeps the fish moist and it browns well; let it cook away toward the last. Serve with any sauce preferred. Is nice with Hollandaise sauce made as follows: One-half cup butter, yolks of two eggs, juice of one-half lemon, one saltspoon salt, few grains cayenne pepper, one-half cup boiling water. Rub butter to a cream, add yolks, one at a time, and beat well; then add lemon juice, salt and pepper. Just before serving add boiling water, stir rapidly till it thickens like custard. Pour sauce around the fish on platter.

BROILED SALT MACKAREL.

S. M. B.

Let the mackarel stand over night in an earthen dish in cold water. When ready to broil, drain. Pour on boiling water and let stand a few minutes, drain and dry with a cloth. Butter the bars of a gridiron. Lay fish on broiler, inside down. Turn for a short time. Serve on a hot platter with plenty of butter.

SAUCE FOR BROILED FISH.

Use in the proportion of one large spoonful of butter to one gill of cream. Turn over fish hot, just before serving.

Why don't you buy your Candies at the Bell Candy Kitchen where they are all home made and fresh. D. Wilson, proprietor, Monmouth, Ill.

TURBOT.

Mrs. Melville Brewer.

Cook white fish until tender. Remove bones, mince fine and add a little chopped celery, sprinkle with salt and pepper. For the dressing, heat one pint of milk and thicken with flour. When cool add two well beaten eggs and one-quarter pound butter. Put in the baking dish a layer of fish then a layer of sauce until the dish is full. Cover the top with cracker crumbs and bake one half hour.

The finest and best Spices at Dunbar's Drug Store.

How to avoid Corns and Bunions.
How to make the Foot Appear Neat.

Where to get Stylish,
Elegantly Made and Durable

Go to **FOOT WEAR,**

J. D. Hickman & Bro., South Main Street. 109

Sign—Big Shoe.   Monmouth, Ill.

The Monmouth Pottery.

Butter Jars of all sizes are made, and a full line of Cooking Ware such as Pudding Pans, Stew Pans, Meat Roasters, Bean Pots, Pie Pans, Coffee and Tea Pots, Etc., Etc.

CROQUETTS.

"Pretty little tiny kickshaws"—*King Henry IV*.

CHICKEN CROQUETTE.
Jessie Weir.

One pint chopped chicken, fine, one-half cup of cream, one-half cup stock, one tablespoonful flour, three tablespoonfuls butter, four eggs, yellow only. Cream the butter and flour, and add to the cream and stock when boiling, then the eggs, well beaten and lemon juice. Work five minutes. Pour over the chicken. Salt and pepper to taste, mix thoroughly. When cold shape into small balls, dip into egg, roll in cracker crumbs and fry in hot lard.

THICK CREAM SAUCE.
Mrs. A. B. Seaman, Denver.

For croquettes and patties. One pint hot cream, two even tablespoon butter, four heaping tablespoon flour, or two heaping tablespoon corn starch, one-half teaspoon salt, one-half saltspoon white pepper, one-half teaspoon celery salt. A few grains of cayenne pepper if desired. Scald the cream, melt the butter in granite sauce pan. When bubbling, add the dry flour, or corn starch, stir till well mixed. Add one-third cream and stir as it boils and thickens. Add more cream and boil again, etc. The sauce should be very thick and smooth. Add the seasoning and mix it while hot with the meat or fish.

C. Shultz for anything in the Drug line.

FILLING FOR PATTIES.
Mrs. Ella Hoyt.

Make a sauce, using one cup of oyster liquor, one tablespoon of butter, one tablespoon of flour, one-half teaspoon anchory essence or paste. Use one pint oysters, one-fourth cup cold water. Wash oysters and remove muscles. Parboil and strain and add to sauce. Season to taste with salt and pepper. ELLA HOYT.

PATTY SHELLS.
K.

One cup butter, one tablespoon white sugar, white of one egg, three tablespoon water, flour enough to roll out. This will make eighteen shells; bake in gem tins.

CREAM SAUCE.
Mrs. Eugene A. Lord.

One pint milk, one tablespoon flour, two tablespoon butter. Salt and pepper. Put butter in a sauce pan, and when hot, but not brown, add the flour. Stir until smooth, then gradually add the milk. Let it boil up once. Season to taste.

SALMON CROQUETTES.
Mrs. E. A. Lord.

One pound chopped salmon, one cup cream, two tablespoonfuls butter, one tablespoonful flour, three eggs, one pint crumbs, pepper and salt to taste. Mix flour and butter together. Let cream come to the boil, and stir in the flour, butter, salmon and seasoning. Boil for one minute. Stir into it one well-beaten egg and remove from the fire. When cold, shape and proceed as for other croquettes.

All the new designs in Artistic, Dining Room and other Wall Papers at McQuiston's.

CHICKEN CROQUETTES.
Mrs. E. A. Lord.

One solid pint of finely chopped chicken, one tablespoon salt, one-half teaspoon of pepper, one cup of cream or chicken stock, one tablespoon flour, four eggs, one teaspoon onion juice, one tablespoon lemon juice, one pint crumbs, three tablespoon butter. Put the cream or stock on to boil in a double boiler. Mix flour and butter together, and stir into the boiling cream, then add the chicken and seasoning. *Boil for two minutes and add two of the eggs, well beaten. Take from the fire immediately and set away to cool. When cold, shape, brush with egg, roll in crumbs and fry.

Veal, mutton, beef and turkey can be prepared in the same manner as chicken. The remains of a veal roast, if tender, is especially good.

RICE CROQUETTES.
Mrs. G. A. Brokaw.

Mix one pint of cold boiled rice with one egg, well beaten; one tablespoon of melted butter, one-half teaspoon salt. Add flour enough to make quite stiff; make in small rolls; then roll them in cracker crumbs, made fine, and fry in hot lard the same as doughnuts.

SALMON CROQUETTES.
Mrs. F. C. Tapping.

One can of salmon, one cup of cracker crumbs, one-third of a lemon, juice and rind. Dressing— Juice of the salmon, one-half cup milk, salt, pepper and small piece of butter, one tablespoon flour. Boil till thick, then mix with the salmon. Roll into small, oblong rolls. Roll in a beaten egg; then in cracker crumbs and fry in lard.

Hodgens' Brick Cream.

VEAL CROQUETTES.
Mrs. John J. Glenn.

Two pounds veal, one cup milk, lump of butter size of walnut, one egg, one tablespoonful flour, one cup rolled crackers. Boil the veal till tender; when cold chop fine, season with pepper and salt. Rub the butter and flour together, place on the fire to melt, add the milk, stir till it thickens, then pour over the meat and mix. When cold make into balls, dip in eggs, roll in the crackers, drop in hot lard, cook till brown. Serve hot.

CHICKEN CROQUETTES.
Mrs. A. B. Seaman, Denver, Col.

Half a pound of chicken chopped fine, and seasoned with salt, pepper, teaspoon of lemon juice and one-half teaspoon chopped parsley. Make one pint of thick cream sauce. When thick add one beaten egg, and mix sauce with the chicken. Make it as soft as can be handled. When cool shape into rolls. Roll in fine bread crumbs, dip in beaten egg, then in crumbs again and fry one minute in smoking hot fat. Mushrooms, boiled rice, sweetbreads, or veal, may be mixed with chicken. Cold roast chicken, chopped fine, may be mixed with the stuffing, moistened with the gravy, and shaped into croquettes.

SALMON CROQUETTES.
Anna Owens.

Two-thirds of a pint of cream, boiling hot, one can salmon. Boil twenty minutes. Pour off the oil and pick to pieces. Add one cup rolled crackers, salt and pepper to taste. Pour the boiling cream and salmon juice over. Prepare as other croquettes.

The finest materials for Cake and Pastry at Dunbar's Drug Store.

JOHN JACOB,

Wholesale and Retail Dealer in

Fresh and Salt Meats, HIDES, ETC.

402 FIFTH AVENUE.

OAKFORD & FAHNESTOCK,
(INCORPORATED.)

Wholesale Grocers,
Tea Importers and Coffee Roasters.

302 and 304 S. Washington and 117, 119, 121 and 123 Liberty Sts,

PEORIA, ILLINOIS.

ASK YOUR GROCER FOR

    Anderson's Jams and Mince-Meat.
    Welsh's Maple Syrup.
    "Blue Ribbon" Canned Goods and Olives.
    Genesee Table Salt.
    Penn Yan "1st Prize" Buckwheat Flour.
    Epicure N. Y. Cheese.

CLARKE & IRVINE,
The Exclusive Grocery Merchants,

Library Block. West Side of the Square.

Study carefully and thoughtfully the wants of the people of Monmouth and vicinity, and will be pleased to serve all that will favor them with their presence. All goods most thoroughly guaranteed.

OYSTERS.

"This treasure of an oyster.'—*Antony and Cleopatra*.

DEVILED OYSTERS.
Mrs. A. B. Seaman.

Twenty-five nice, fat oysters, one half-pint cream, one tablespoon butter, two tablespoons flour, one tablespoon chopped parsley, yolks of two eggs. Salt and pepper to taste. Drain the oysters, chop them middling fine, and drain again. Put the milk on to boil. Rub the butter and flour together and stir into milk when boiling. As soon as it thickens, take it from the fire and add the other ingredients. Beat yolks before adding them. Have the deep shells of the oysters washed clean, fill them with this mixture, sprinkle bread crumbs on top. Put shells in dripping pan and brown in quick oven for five minutes. Serve in shells or bake dishes. Avoid long cooking, it makes them dry.

CREAMED OYSTERS.
Mrs. Ella Porter, Hanna.

One pint cream, one heaping tablespoon butter, two heaping teaspoon flour, one-half teaspoon salt, one-half saltspoon pepper, cayenne and celery salt. Melt the butter, add flour, then the boiling milk, or cream, and seasoning. To this add one quart oysters, parboiled, Turn into a baking dish, cover with cracker crumbs and bake in a quick oven—or serve on toast.

C. Shults' Drug and Fine Perfumery

OYSTER PATTIES.
Mrs Dr. Kimmel.

Make puff paste in this way: To every pound of flour add three-fourths of a pound of butter, the yolk of one egg; use ice cold water; chop half the butter into the flour, then stir in the egg; work all into a dough; roll out thin; spread on some of the butter, fold closely (butter side in) and roll again; do this until the butter is all used up. Keep the paste in a cool place while you prepare the oysters. Set the oysters on the stove with liquid enough to cover them. As soon as they come to a boil skim them, stir in a little butter and pepper, also, if desired, a little cream. Line your small tins with the paste; put three or four oysters in each, add a little of the liquor, then cover with paste. Bake in a quick oven twenty minutes. While hot wash over the top with a beaten egg.

OYSTER IN VINEGAR.
K.

Heat the oysters in their own liquor for a few minutes, then drop into hot vinegar, with butter, pepper and salt to taste.

LITTLE PIGS IN BLANKETS.
Mrs. Joseph Stevenson, Omaha.

Wash large oysters and dry thoroughly. Have slices of bacon cut very thin. Salt and pepper oysters. Pin on each, with wooden toothpick a slice of bacon, and broil or bake until the bacon is crisp. Serve hot, without removing the toothpick.

ESCALLOPED OYSTERS.
Mrs. Babcock, Denver.

To one quart of oysters take two-thirds of a cup of butter and the same of flour, rub the flour and

Hodgens' Lemon Ice.

butter to cream, and stir into one pint of boiling milk. Stir the oysters ifi the sauce while boiling hot. Season with salt and pepper, Cover with rolled crackers, place in oven and bake.

OYSTER PIE.
M.

Two cans of oysters, or three pints of solid oysters, one quart of cream, one dozen rolled crackers. Pepper and salt. Stir all together, and pour into a dish lined with thick puff paste. Cover with another paste and bake three-quarters of an hour. This is a delicious mode of cooking oysters.

OYSTER FRITTERS.
Mrs. W. D. Bell.

Strain the oysters and remove all bits of shell. Cut the oysters slightly. For a pint of oysters use a pint of flour, sifted and mixed with a level teaspoon of salt. Put the flour in a mixing bowl with the yolk of one egg, a teaspoon of salad oil (butter if you prefer) and a pinch of pepper. Use enough of the oyster liquor to make a batter thick enough to drop from the spoon. Beat the white of the egg to a stiff froth. Mix the oysters and the white of egg lightly with the batter and as soon as mixed drop by the large spoonful into a kettle of hot lard and fry a nice brown. Lay a brown paper on a dripping pan and take fritters out on this to drain. Set in the oven to keep hot while frying the rest.

FRIED OYSTERS.
Georgie Dennis.

Roll and sift crackers, and beat egg very light. Dip oysters in egg then in sifted cracker, again in the egg and last in the cracker. Fry in hot lard till brown. Pepper and salt to taste.

Hodgens' Ice Cream.

FRIED OYSTERS.
Mrs. Edgar MacDill.

Drain and remove all bits of shell. Sprinkle with salt and pepper. Set in a cool place for ten minutes. Then pour oysters into a pan of crackers, rolled fine. Add liquor. Mix well and let stand five minutes. Add a little salt and pepper. Mold into small cakes with two or three oysters in each cake. Roll in dry cracker and fry in butter. Serve hot. Use just enough cracker to hold the oysters together. If there is not sufficient liquor to moisten cracker, use milk.

FILLING FOR PATTIES.
C. B.

Breasts of two chickens, one can mushrooms, two cups cream, two teaspoon butter, three teaspoon flour, one of chopped parsley, and a little mustard. Boil chicken and mushrooms separately, chop in small pieces. Rub butter and flour together, stir into cream and boil until it thickens, then pour this over chicken and mushrooms and fill shells.

OYSTER PATTIES.
Mrs. John Babcock.

One pint of small oysters, one-half pint of cream, a large teaspoon of flour, salt and pepper. Let the cream come to a boil. Mix the flour with a little cold milk, and stir into the boiling cream. Season with salt and pepper while the cream is cooking. Let the oysters come to a boil in their own liquor. Skim carefully and drain off all the liquor. Add oysters to cream and boil up once. Fill the patty shells and serve. The quantities given are enough for eighteen shells.

Nail, Hand, Teeth and Hair Brushss at Dunbar's Drug Store.

ESCALLOPED OYSTERS.
Mrs. J. B. McMichael.

Roll crackers, not too fine. Drain liquor from one quart of oysters. Butter a deep dish or pan. Cover the bottom with crackers, put in a layer of oysters, pepper and salt and bits of butter. Another layer of crackers, then oysters, until the dish is filled, having crackers cover top. Pour over the liquor from oysters and a pint of milk. Bake three-quarters of an hour in Monmouth Pottery Pudding Pan.

C. Shultz' for anything in the Drug line.

N. A. SCOTT,

PIONEER GROCERY,

Wholesale and Retail Grocer,

Southeast Corner Square and Market Place.
MONMOUTH. ILLINOIS.

J. C. Hanna. Pres't.   J. E. Jackson. V.-Pres't.   P. L. Sherrick. Sec'y and Treas.   W. P. Cleaver, Gen'l Manager.

SHERRICK-CLEAVER CO.

Manufacturers of

Shirts, Pants, Overalls, Etc., Etc.

SPECIALTIES--Cassimere Pants
and Duck Coats.   MONMOUTH, ILLINOIS.

"A Contented Mind is a Continual Feast."

The surest way to secure composure and serenity is by being well dressed; hence consult

WARREN BUNKERR,

THE DISTINGUISHED GENTLEMAN

MILLINER AND DRESSMAKER,

Who has just returned from Paris, and furnishes all the correct fashions and latest novelties.

OSCAR ZIMMERMAN,

GENERAL BARBER SUPPLIES

Sole Proprietor   ) Refreshing   (
of the ......   ) Delightful   (DISTILLED HAZEL BAY.

Pinaud Toilet Waters, Perfumes, Etc., Etc.

Finest Grinding and Decorating Establishment west of Chicago. Get your carving, cake and bread knives, razors and shears sharpened.

MEATS.

"Dainty bits make—to the ribs."

HOW TO ROAST MEAT.

Mrs. Emma P. Ewing, of the school of domestic economy at the Iowa Agricultural College, says :
In roasting meats of all kinds the method adopted should be the one that in the most perfect manner preserves the juices inside the meat. To roast beef in the best possible manner, place the clean cut side of the meat upon a smoking hot pan, which must be over a quick fire. Press it close to the pan until seared and slightly browned. Reverse and let the opposite side become similarly seared and browned. Then put it at once in the oven, the heat of which should be firm and steady, but not too intense, and leave it undisturbed until cooked. The time that should be allowed for cooking beef in this manner is twenty minutes to the pound, if it is to be rare, less half an hour deducted from the aggregate time on account of searing. In other words, a five-pound roast of beef will require an hour and a quarter, a six-pound roast an hour and a half, and so on.

If the oven is not too hot the beef requires no basting, and is better without it. When the oven is at the proper temperature, and the cooking is going on all right, the meat will keep up a gentle sputtering in the pan. If, upon opening the oven door, this sputtering is not perceptible, more heat

Hodgens' Pine Apple Ice.

is required. But, if in addition to the sputtering, any smoke is discernable in the oven, the heat is too intense, and should be lessened. Unless the heat of the oven is too great, the drippings in the pan will burn and smoke, and when the meat is cooked there will be a thin coating of brown jelly in the pan where the meat rested, which, by the addition of stock or water, will make a delicious gravy.

A roast of beef should never be washed, and if it has been accidentally wet or moistened, it should be carefully wiped dry before it is seared or put to cook. Searing almost instantly coats the cut side of a piece of meat, and prevents the escape of juices in the after-process of roasting, while a firm, steady heat gently but thoroughly cooks it, and thus both juices and flavor are preserved. Basting is a troublesome, as well as a damaging, process. And as salt and water have a tendency to toughen and extract the juices of meat, they should not be used on it while roasting, if it is desired to have the meat sweet, juicy and tender.

ROAST BEEF.
M.

The best pieces for roasting are the sirloin and rib pieces. When roasting in an oven dash a cup of hot water over the meat; this checks the escape of the juices. Baste frequently with salt, and water and the drippings. If your fire is hot, allow twelve minutes to the pound, if you like the beef rare; more if you prefer it well done. Thicken the gravy with browned flour.

THE MOST DELICATE FLAVORS ARE OBTAINED FROM CHICAGO FLAVORING EXTRACTS.

TO ROAST BEEF.
M.

Put into pan without water, unless in gasoline stove oven, when put in sufficient water to keep from burning. Do not season. Allow twelve minutes to a pound for a rare roast, longer if it is desired better done. Make gravy in usual way. The best way ever roasted.

GRAVY FOR TURKEY.
B. M.

An excellent way to roast turkey. Wash thoroughly and wipe dry. Do not salt. Fill with dressing Put without water in double roaster. Do not baste. Keep fire enough to hear a gentle sizzle. Bake twenty minutes for each pound. One and one-half hours before it is done pour over a gravy made of three large cups boiling water, three tablespoons flour, first mixed with small quantity of water and one-half cup of butter and salt to taste. This gives sufficient moisture to the turkey and makes delicious gravy, rich and brown,

A good dressing may be made of bread crumbs, butter, pepper and salt, nutmeg, sage, and onions if desired, well buttered slices of bread. Make about right proportion.

Chicken is excellent baked in this way. Allowing at least twenty minutes to each pound.

POT ROAST OF BEEF.
B.

Take four pounds ribbed beef, ribs taken out and rolled. Put some beef drippings in porcelain-lined kettle, rub beef with salt and put it into the hot drippings. Let it cook one hour, turning it frequently, then add water and cook one hour longer. Re-

---

The finest Soaps and Perfumes at John C. Dunbar's Drug Store.

move to platter and thicken the gravy with flour
and butter made into a paste.

GOOD STEAK.
Mrs. Dr. W. P. Smith.

In the first place buy *good* steak—porterhouse—
have it cut *two inches thick* ; remove all the bone
and most of the fat, put the steak upon a heavy
hard wood block and with an iron beater—2 inch
face and 36 sharp teeth, (mine weighs 2 ℔s.)—
bring the meat to *one-half an inch in thickness*.
For a gridiron use a large double bread toaster ;
open this and place the steak upon one side, adjusted to the thickness you desire it when broiled;
close down the other half of toaster, pushing the
slide clear up, to fasten the meat at the proposed
thickness, place this over a bed of very hot coals
for about ten seconds—this seals the surface and
prevents the juicees running—turn it and cook the
other side done, slightly browning it ; then turn
the first side and cook that the same—steak should
be broiled quick, and is best if not overdone, but
so that when cut 'tis very juicy and a little red in
centre—unclose the handles of your broiler and
with forks remove your steak to a hot platter,
season nicely with salt and pepper, and place
about the surface small pieces of butter, put it in
the oven long enough to melt this, then to the
table, and it is ready for the carver.

SPICED BEEF.
Mrs. B.

Take a piece of beef from the fore quarter,
weighing ten pounds—those who like fat should
select a fatty piece, those who prefer lean may
take the shoulder clod or the upper part of the

C. Shultz for anything in the Drug line.

fore leg—take one pint of salt, one teacup of molasses or brown sugar, and tablespoon of ground cloves, allspice and pepper, and two tablespoons of pulverized saltpetre; place the beef in a deep pan, rub with this mixture, turn and rub each side twice a day for a week, then wash off the spices, put in a pot of boiling water, and, as often as it boils hard, turn in a teacupful of cold water; it must must simmer for five hours on the back part of the stove; press under a heavy weight till it is cold and you will never desire to try corned beef of the butcher again, your pickle will do for another ten pounds of beef, first rubbing into it a handful of salt, it can be renewed and a piece kept in preparation every day.

TO BROIL A STEAK, CHICKENS, GAME OR FISH IN THE OVEN.
K. C. S.

Place the meats in a double wire broiler, put the broiler over the baking pan containing an inch of cold water, place the pan on the top shelf of the oven, which should be very hot—for sirloin steak, from eight to ten minutes, other articles according to size and heat of the oven.

SPICED ROAST.
Mrs. J. A. Hanna.

For this either beef or mutton can be used. Prepare for roasting by seasoning with salt and pepper, then add one half-dozen whole cloves, one dozen whole allspice, 3 tablespoons sugar, one-third pint vinegar and two-thirds water; roast very slowly until about a half hour before serving,

---

Hodgens' Tuty Fruty Cream.

when let it brown in a very hot oven. Baste often and add water as needed.

SPRING CHICKEN.

Take a nice spring chicken, or a young one. Clean and wash thoroughly and put in a kettle with a pint and a half of cold water. Let it boil twenty minutes, or until tender, but not until it falls to pieces. Take out of the water. Save the water for the gravy. Split open the chicken on the back. Put in a dripping pan, add salt and pepper and little pieces of butter. Then dredge it with flour, allowing some of the flour to fall into pan. Put into a hot oven and brown. Watch it, and after it has been in ten minutes—for if the chicken is young it takes only a few minutes—thirty at the most. Take out of pan and put on a platter. Take the stock, thicken and put it into the dripping pan where the chicken has just been taken out, and cook it until smooth, stirring constantly. It ought to be brown if some of the flour and butter that the chicken was baked in was left. Lastly, pour over the chicken and serve hot. If one has an old fowl it must be boiled or hour or two before it will be tender enough to split opn.

JELLIED CHICKEN.
Mary Patterson.

Boil a fowl until it will slip easily from the bones, let the water be reduced to about one pint in boiling. Pick the meat from the bones in good sized pieces, taking out all gristle, fat and bones. Place in a wet mold, skim the fat from the liquor. A little butter, pepper and salt to the taste, and one-half ounce of gelatine. When this dissolves pour it hot over the chicken. The liquor must be seasoned pretty high, for the chicken absorbs.

Hodgens' Salted Almonds.

TO COOK VEAL LIVER.
Mrs. S.

Pour boiling water over it, put a tablespoon of lard and butter in frying pan, lay the liver in, chop fine two small onions, cover the liver with them, sprinkle with flour, salt and pepper, cover closely, and let it fry for a few minutes, then turn and salt and pepper the on other side. With ease it can be sent to the table with the dressing on each slice, which adds very much to the relish.

FOR CORNING BEEF OR TONGUES.
Mrs. Frank Hubbard.

To one gallon of water take one and one-half pounds of salt, one half-pound of sugar, one-half ounce of saltpetre. Boil these together and skim when cold, pour it over your meat or tongues and let it stand two weeks before boiling. A large tongue will take five hours to cook tender.

NO. 2.—CORNED BEEF OR HAM.

Seven pounds salt, three pounds brown sugar, four ounces saltpetre, two ounces soda and two gallons of water. Boil and skim well and turn on meat when cold. Let them remain three or four weeks before using.

CREAM SWEET BREAD.
M.

Always get calves' sweet breads. They should be soaked from one to three hours in salt water, and boil twenty minutes, then throw in cold water for five minutes. Then remove all skin and rough parts, cut in small pieces, make cream sauce, put the sweetbreads in the sauce and let them get very hot then put in small dishes and cover with crumbs and little bits of butter. Put in oven and brown.

CHICAGO YEAST POWDER IS GUARANTEED HIGHEST QUALITY, AND COSTS LESS THAN ANY OTHER.

SWEETBREADS ON TOAST.
S.

Cook as above, dress with cream sauce and pour very hot over buttered toast.

SWEETBREADS FRIED.

After laying in salted water put them in cold water a few minutes, then dry in a cloth, fry them with little strips of salt pork, or dip in beaten egg and roll in bread crumbs and fry in hot lard. Pour over half a cup of rich cream, stir in one teaspoon flour, let it boil up a few minutes and serve hot.

VEAL CUTLETS OR STEAK.

Cut in pieces ready to serve, roll in bread or cracker crumbs seasoned with salt, pepper—and summer savory if desired—after dipping in beaten egg; have plenty of butter and lard in equal parts; fry quickly on one side then turn and cook thoroughly. A gravy may be made of flour and cream if desired, and either poured over meat or served in boat.

BAKED HAM.

Take ham, ten or twelve pounds, wash and trim off uneven fat. Make a paste of rye flour that will spread nicely, spread over all the flesh of ham exposed. Put in a roaster on rack or plate, bake from three to four hours even heat. When done peel off the paste and rind and stick cloves in to flavor.

VEAL LOAF.
Mabel Pillsbury.

Boil two pounds lean veal. When cold chop fine with one-fourth pound salt pork. Add four butter crackers rolled fine, two eggs, well beaten, three hard-boiled eggs sliced thin, two teaspoons

---

C. Shultz', Drugs and Fine Perfumery.

salt, one saltspoon pepper, one-half teaspoon nutmeg. Put in baking mold. Pour over it the meat liquor until it stands on the top. Cover with cracker crumbs and bake one hour.

VEAL A LA POULETTE.
Mrs. A. G. VanHoorebeke.

Take of the breast of veal, cut it up in pieces about two inches square, put it on to stew with a little water, salt, pepper and just a little grated nutmeg, stew slowly for two hours, add a piece of butter and the juice of a small lemon, then thicken the gravy with the yolk of eggs, taking care not to let it curdle.

VEAL LOAF.
Mrs. J. R. Ebersole.

Three pounds of raw veal chopped very fine, butter the size of an egg, three eggs, three tablespoons cream or milk, if milk use a small piece of butter, mix the eggs and cream together, mix with the veal four pounded crackers, one teaspoon black pepper, one large tablespoon salt, one large tablespoon sage. Mix well together and form into a loaf. Bake two and a half hours, basting with butter and water while baking. Serve cut in thin slices.

VEAL LOAF.
M. B. Sexton.

Three pounds of veal chopped fine, one-quarter pound of salt pork or equal quantity of butter, one cup pounded crackers, two well beaten eggs, one-half teaspoon black pepper, one-half teaspoon salt, one tablespoon sage, one-fourth of a nutmeg, juice of one lemon. Mix and press into a bread pan. Bake two hours and eat cold.

Hodgens' for anything in the Party line.

JELLIED VEAL.

Mrs. H. Smith.

Chop veal fine and salt to taste. Add to one pint of any soup stock a quarter box of gelatine, salt, pepper and nutmeg to taste. Take two hard boiled eggs and one lemon, slice thin, line mould with lemon and eggs, fill with the chopped meat and bits of lemon and egg, pour over all the soup stock and set away to cool. Chicken or turkey may be used the same way.

ROAST SPICED MUTTON.

Mrs. B.

Take a leg of mutton. Pound it well to make tender, rub well with salt, make gashes all over it into which put small pieces of salt pork, onion, whole pepper and cloves. Brown in hot oven without water, when brown add water and baste often, cook two and one-half hours, thicken gravy with flour before serving. Chop two pickles fine and add to the gravy.

VEAL LOAF.

Linnie Brewer

Three pounds of veal, one pound of pork. Have all chopped fine at the butchers. Roll three square crackers, keep out a little for the outside, a half cup butter (don't use quite all), two eggs beaten, one-half cup of water, one tablespoon of salt, one teaspoon of pepper. Mix all well together, form in a nice loaf, make it firm, put in a long, narrow pan. Put the remaining cracker and butter over the top, a little water and bake two and one-half hours, basting once in a while with hot water and butter.

C. Shultz', Drugs and Fine Perfumery.

SCRAPLE.
Mrs. Flora Hyde.

Take a hog's head, heart, tongue and part of the liver. Cleanse thoroughly and soak in salt water twenty-four hours. Put on to boil in cold water. Cook until all the bones can be easily removed. Then take out in a chopping bowl and chop fine. Season highly with sage, salt and pepper. Return it to the liquor on the stove, which you must strain. Then thicken with corn meal and a tea-cup of buckwheat flour till the consistency of mush. Then dip out in deep dishes, and when cool slice and fry a rich brown, as you would mush. It is very nice for a cold morning breakfast. If you make more than you can use at once, run hot lard over the rest and you can keep it all through the winter.

MEAT BALLS.
Mrs. A. J. Waid.

Take pieces of cooked meat, fat and lean, that have been left over and put them through the meat chopper, or chop them very fine in a wooden bowl. To about a pint of this meat add two beaten eggs, a handful or two of rolled crackers. Pepper and salt to taste. Stir all together and add water to make it moist enough to form into ·flat balls. Grease the frying pan and cook lightly.

TO SEASON SAUSAGE
Mrs. Sarah Ruse.

For ten pounds of pork, one-third fat, two-thirds lean, when ground, use ten teaspoons salt, five teaspoons pepper, three teaspoons of pulverized sage.

Hodgens' Candy.

FOR CURING MEAT.
Mrs. Wylie.

Ten quarts salt, three pounds brown sugar, one pound pepper, three-fourths pound saltpetre. This amount is for 100 pounds meat. Mix all together in a tub and then rub the meat thoroughly with it and lay it on plank and leave for three weeks unless the weather is very cold, and then it can be left longer.

VEAL LOAF.
Mrs. Jno. Brewer.

For three pounds use two eggs, beaten light, four crackers rolled fine, leave out enough to roll it in. One teaspoon pepper and one teaspoon of salt. Butter size of an egg. melted. Mix all together. Bake two or two and a half hours, according to heat of oven. Baste often with the water. Take out of the oven a half hour before dinner.

FRIED CHICKEN.
Mrs. Eliza B Smith.

Cut the chicken in pieces. Wipe dry. Salt to taste. Roll each piece in flour. Use bacon frying and lard equal parts. If butter is used with lard, use only enough to make brown nicely. Have your grease hot, and cook slowly, turning until nicely browned from the grease, and add a little water and cover. Let steam. Make gravy.

IN-EVERY RECIPE WHERE BAKING POWDER IS REQUIRED USE **CHICAGO YEAST POWDER.**

Liverpool.   Ottumwa.   Chicago.

John Morrell & Co.,
Limited.

Pork Packers, Provision Dealers.

The "Iowa's Pride" brand of Hams and Bacon are not excelled by any in flavor or appearance. Call for "Iowa's Pride" Ham, Iowa's Pride Breakfast Bacon, Iowa's Pride Special Breakfast Bacon. Be sure to see that our name is burned on the skin.

Morrell's Pure Lard

Warranted free from all adulteration, is the lard for you to use. Call for it and have no other. Also try "Wapello" brand of Breakfast Bacon, "Dove" brand Breakfast Bacon, "California" Hams, Shoulders, and Pickled goods Call for these brands and get honest, reliable goods for your money. Handled by all first-class grocers and Butchers.

J. W. SIPHER,   J. D. DIFFENBAUGH,
Pres.   *Sec'y and Treas.*

1869-1894.

Sipher Lumber and Coal Co,

Lumber, Coal and Ice, Sash, Doors and Blinds.

617 S Second Street—Telephone No. 6,
Monmouth, Ill.

The Very Best Receipt of all

Will be one for

The Republican

For one Year, $1.50. It would give enjoyment for 365 days.

VEGETABLES.

"Unquiet meals make ill digestion."—*Comedy of Errors.*

FRIED APPLES.
S.

Slice unpared apples about one-half of an inch thick. Fry slowly in butter or good drippings. When done sprinkle with sugar and serve very hot. Nice at breakfast, or served with pork.

ASPARAGUS ON TOAST.

Cut asparagus in small pieces. Boil in salted water. When done dress with cream, or milk and butter, and pour over well buttered hot toast.

ASPARAGUS IN OMELETTE.
K. C.

Well cooked asparagus chopped and mixed with omelette before frying is very palatable.

BOSTON BAKED BEANS.
Mrs. Wildemuth.

One quart of beans soaked over night. Cook one-half hour. One desertspoon New Orleans molasses, one teaspoon ground mustard. Salt and pepper to taste. Small piece of salt pork. Bake six hours in Monmouth Pottery Bean Pots.

BOSTON BAKED BEANS.
Mrs. Carrie Dearborn, Boston.

One pound of small white beans. Wash well and soak over night. Parboil until tender, but not

Hodgens' Orange Ice.

soft. Strain and wash with cold water. Put in baking pot and add tablespoon of salt, small piece onion, teaspoon of mustard, one-fourth cup of molasses, or two tablespoons of sugar. Cover one-half pound of salt pork with beans, pour in boiling water sufficient to nearly cover the beans. Cover closely and bake slowly eight hours. Remove cover half an hour before serving to let beans brown.

ESCALLOPED CABBAGE.

Put a head of cabbage washed and chopped into boiling water, and boil twenty minutes. Drain in a colander, place in two baking dishes and pour over it a sauce made as follows : Melt four tablespoons of butter and add four level teaspoons of flour, stirring together until blended, then add one quart of milk and stir constantly until it boils, then add six hard boiled eggs which have been chopped fine, two teaspoons of salt, and a dash of pepper. Pour this over the cabbage, sprinkle with bread crumbs, moistened with melted butter, and bake in a quick oven fifteen minutes. The proportions are sufficient for two dishes and will serve ten or twelve persons.

CREAM CABBAGE.
Mrs. F. E. Campbell.

Slice cabbage fine. Put in hot salted water to boil. There should be more than enough water to cover cabbage. Just before it is soft drain, and add for one small cabbage, about two teaspoons of flour, butter size of an egg, one teacup milk or cream. With cream use less butter. Pepper and salt to taste. Let cook for a few minutes.

Hodgens' Brick Cream and Flavors.

ESCALLOPED CAULIFLOWER.
Mrs. E. A. Lord.

Cook the cauliflower one hour in salt and water. Drain and break apart. Put a layer of the cauliflower in an escalop dish, moisten it with cream sauce and sprinkle in a little grated cheese. Put in another layer of cauliflower, and continue, as directed before, until all the vegetable is used. There should be two tablespoons of grated cheese and one pint of sauce to each head of cauliflower. Cover with bread crumbs and cheese and dot with bits of butter. Bake half an hour in moderate oven.

CELERY.
B.

Wash. Cut in pieces about one inch long. Boil one and a half to two hours. Drain. Add cream or milk. Milk, butter, pepper and salt, as for peas.

ESCALLOPED CABBAGE.
Mrs. I. M. Eastam.

Cut one-half head of cabbage fine and stew until tender. Dress with milk, butter, pepper and salt. Put a layer of cabbage and one of rolled crackers in a pan until the pan is full. Add milk, butter, pepper and salt, as you would for oysters. Put in oven and bake twenty minutes.

BAKED CORN.

Put layer of cracker crumbs in baking dish, then layer of corn—the canned will do just as well. Butter, salt and pepper, then another layer of crumbs and corn. Pour over cream or milk. Bake one-half to three-fourths of an hour. Add milk to keep moist.

Hodgens' Restaurant.

VEGETABLES.

CORN OYSTERS
Margaret Dunbar.

To one quart grated corn, add three eggs and three or four grated crackers, beat well and season with pepper and salt. Have ready in skillet butter and lard, or beef drippings in equal proportions, hot but not scorching. Drop in little cakes about the size of an oyster (using a teaspoon for the purpose). When brown turn and fry on other side, being very careful that they do not burn. Serve hot. The white of the eggs should be beaten to a stiff froth and added just before frying. When green corn is out of season, canned corn or "kornlet" may be used.

ESCALLOPED POTATOES.
Mrs. J. A. Brundage.

Boil potatoes until tender in their jackets, then peel and slice them in a basin; put a layer of potatoes, sprinkled with pepper, salt and a little flour, a small piece of butter, then another layer of potatoes, then seasoning until your basin is filled; then fill your basin half full of milk and bake half an hour.

EGG PLANT.—No. 2.
Anna Brady.

Peel the egg plant, boil until done, then pour off the water, mash fine; pepper, butter and salt to taste; put in a shallow pudding pan, and over the top place a thick layer of cracker crumbs. Bake half an hour in a moderate oven.

CORN FRITTERS OR MOCK OYSTERS.
Palmer House, Chicago.

Grate six ears of corn, and mix with one tablespoon flour, two eggs. Salt and pepper to taste. Drop spoonfuls in hot lard and fry like oysters.

THE MOST DELICATE FLAVORS ARE OBTAINED FROM **CHICAGO FLAVORING EXTRACTS.**

VEGETABLES.

CORN FRITTERS.
Mrs. Amanda White.

One pint of canned corn. Half a teacup of milk, two eggs beaten well, one tablespoon of melted butter, one teaspoon of salt, two heaping teaspoons of baking powder, a half cup of sifted flour and a little pepper. Mix all together, stirring only enough to get the ingredients well mixed. Fry in hot lard, but do not have the pan too hot, or the fritters will brown too quickly on the outside and not puff up nicely. Drop them into the frying pan from the point of a spoon and fry a light brown on both sides.

LYONAISE POTATOES.
C. K.

Fry one medium sized onion chopped very fine, in a tablespoon of butter ; chop fine cold boiled potatoes and put in skillet with onions. Fry a light brown, stirring constantly. Add two tablespoons parsley to potatoes.

EGG PLANT.—No. 1.
Anna Brady.

Peel and cut in slices the purple kind, sprinkle with salt and let drain for one hour; make a light batter with one egg, flour and a little water, dip the slices into it and fry in butter.

SACKED POTATOES.
Mrs. Jos. Stevenson.

Select for baking, potatoes as near of a size as possible. When baked, cut off one end, scrape out the inside with a spoon, being careful not to break the skins. Add to the potatoes, butter, salt and sufficient hot milk to make quite soft. Fill the skins with this and place on end in a buttered pan and bake until brown on top. The potatoes will puff up considerably if sufficiently beaten. Nice for breakfast or tea.

BAKED TURNIPS.
S. I.

If large, split, and bake as you would potatoes, only longer—two or three hours if large. When done, mash fine, season with butter, salt and pepper. Serve hot.

MUSHROOM OMELET

To one can mushrooms take twelve or sixteen eggs. Cook mushrooms in their own liquor till tender. When cold chop rather fine. Season with salt and pepper. To the eggs, well beaten, add mushrooms, and when ready to serve, scramble in the old-fashioned way, only very soft, adding a little butter.

POTATOES STEWED IN BUTTER.

Peel the potatoes and slice them into rather small, even slices; put them over the fire in enough salted boiling water to cover them, and boil until they begin to grow tender, but not until they begin to break; drain, and to a pint of potatoes, used about two heaping tablespoons of butter and a scant half cup of milk. When the butter is melted and put with the milk, put in the potatoes and shake gently to keep from sticking to the pan, being careful not to break them until they have absorbed the butter and milk; season to taste with salt and white pepper.

MACARONI.
Mrs. R. M. Stevenson, Tarkio, Mo.

Put macaroni on stove with water to cover for one half hour. Heat one pint of milk, stir in two or three well beaten eggs, salt macaroni, put all together, grate a little cheese on top with pieces of butter all around. Bake from twenty to thirty minutes.

Do not take medicine when you are well.

ESCALLOPED TOMATOES.

Grease well with butter a pudding dish and place the first layer of crushed crackers, butter, pepper and salt and a little water, and the next layer of ripe tomatoes with a little butter, pepper and salt until the dish is full, the last layer being of crackers and seasoning. Canned tomatoes may be used.

ESCALLOPED ONIONS.
H. K.

For three persons, peel and boil three good sized onions; when tender chop and place in baking dish with alternate layers of bread crumbs; season with butter, pepper and salt, and moisten thoroughly with milk; bake.

MACARONI AND TOMATOES.

Break a cupful of macaroni into pieces an inch long and boil twenty minutes, after soaking an hour in plenty of cold water and washing well. Make a puree of one quart of tomatoes and one small onion. Add a lump of butter the size of an egg, salt and pepper and sugar, if you like; drain the macaroni and add; serve hot.

STEWED MACARONI.

Boil two ounces of macaroni in water, drain well, put into a saucepan one ounce of butter, mix with one tablespoon of flour, moisten with four tablespoons of veal or beef stock, one gill of cream; salt and pepper to taste; put in macaroni, let it boil up and serve while hot.

PARSNIPS.
B.

Boil with thin slices of bacon. Allow the water to boil off and fry down to rich brown. The bacon gives fine flavor.

Sunshine is one of nature's most potent remedies.

VEGETABLES.

GREEN TOMATOES FRIED.

Take four large, smooth, green tomatoes; slice; let stand in cold salt water for a half hour; drain and dredge well with flour, salt and pepper and fry in butter, a nice brown; serve hot.

BAKED TOMATOES.
Mrs. M. J. B.

Cut a thin slice from the blossom side of the tomatoes and with a teaspoon remove the pulp without breaking the shell; chop one onion and add, with bread crumbs rubbed fine, to the pulp and season with pepper and salt (and sugar, if you like). When thoroughly mixed fill the tomatoes and put the slice back in its place. Put in baking dish, stem side down with just a little water and a lump of butter on each to keep from burning.

VEGETABLE OYSTER PLANT.
Mrs. C. C. Pollard.

Scrape plant, cut into crosswise slices, and put into boiling water and boil until tender, then thicken with cracker or bread crumbs, mash fine, season with butter, pepper and salt. Have ready a skillet with two tablespoons of hot lard, drop in cakes and fry until brown.

POTATO PUFFS.
Mrs. C. C. McCoy.

One cup mashed potato, one cup milk, one egg, two teaspoons baking powder, flour to mix soft; roll and cut in strips about size of finger and roll lightly with the hand and fry as you would doughnuts; eat warm with butter or syrup.

POTATO BALLS.
P.

Mix mashed potatoes with the yolk of one egg, roll them into balls, flour them or roll in egg and bread crumbs, and fry a light brown in good drippings.

VEGETABLES.

FRIED PARSNIPS.
M. P.

Peel and boil; when done, drain, season with pepper and salt, dip first in melted butter, then in flour, and dust with sugar. Put two tablespoons of drippings or lard into a frying pan; when hot put in enough parsnips to cover bottom of pan, fry brown on one side, then turn and brown on the other. Serve with roast pork.

POTATO PEARS.
Mrs. Patterson.

Mash and season one half dozen potatoes. Mold them while warm into the shape of small pears, dip them in the beaten yolk of egg, stick in the small end of each pear a clove (the large end of the clove in the potato), to represent the stem. Bake in a quick oven fifteen or twenty minutes till a rich brown. Success depends on thorough mashing and seasoning, and baking long enough to heat them through.

POTATO PUFFS.
Mrs. B.

Two cups mashed potatoes, two tablespoons melted butter beaten until creamy, then add two well beaten eggs and one cup of cream, a little salt, beat well, pour into a baking dish, spread butter over the top and bake quickly a delicate brown.

FRIED SWEET POTATOES.
Mrs. Mary A. Frantz.

Boil or steam the potatoes until almost done. When ready to fry pare them, cut in slices one-fourth of an inch thick. Take butter the size of an egg, four tablespoons sugar, put into frying pan; when all is melted lay in potatoes; have a moderate fire; when brown, turn; fry without cover.

C. Shultz' for anything in the Drug line.

ONION PIE.
Mrs. Pen D. Good.

Take one dozen onions, cut up and put in a skillet with butter and lard and fry till soft; then add half cup of sweet cream, half cup of milk, two eggs, and thicken it with a little paste made of milk and flour; then season with pepper and salt; bake the pie crust first and have ready; when you get the onions all done, put in the baked crust and set in oven long enough to brown on top.

ONIONS.

This healthful vegetable should be eaten oftener and would be if it were not for the disagreeable odor. The following way of preparing modifies this and prevents the burning sensation often felt in the stomach. Slice very thin, pour over boiling water, let them stand five minutes or longer, serve with a very little vinegar and salt; excellent with salad dressing.

HOW TO BOIL RICE.

Pick your rice clean and wash it in two cold waters, not draining off the last water until you are ready to put the rice on the fire. Prepare a saucepan with water and a little salt. When it boils sprinkle in the rice gradually so as not to stop the boiling. Boil hard for twenty minutes, keeping the pot covered. Then take it from the fire and pour off the water, after which set the pot on the back of the stove with the lid off to allow the rice to dry and the grains to separate.

Remember—Boil rapidly from the time you cover the pot until you take it off; this allows each grain to swell to three times its normal size and the motion prevents the grains from sticking together. Don't stir it as this will cause it to fall to the bottom and burn. When properly boiled, rice should be snowy white, perfectly dry and soft, and every grain separate and alone.

Ask your grocer for Anderson's Jams and Mincemeats

MACARONI AND CHEESE.
E.

Break in pieces, boil about an hour in plenty of water, adding more as it soaks into macaroni; put in baking dish with alternate layers of grated cheese; salt; nearly cover mith milk. Bake half hour; a beaten egg may be added.

ESCALLOPED MUSHROOMS.

Put the mushrooms in a buttered baking dish with alternate layers of crumbs, seasoning each layer plentifully with butter; add salt, pepper and a gill of cream or gravy. Bake twenty minutes, keeping covered while in the oven.

TOMATOES AND RICE.
Mrs. E. Jamieson.

In cooking tomatoes for one half dozen persons, put in two tablespoons of raw rice when first put on to stew. It will be found a very palatable dish cooked until the rice is well done, and seasoned with butter, pepper and salt.

TOMATO FRITTERS.
Mrs. E.

One pint stewed tomatoes, one egg, half teaspoon soda, flour enough to make the batter the consistency of pancakes.

CANNED PEAS.
French Cook.

Treat any good canned peas in following manner and they will be found nearly equal to fresh ones: Turn from can into colander and drain off liquor. Then put in plenty of salted hot water and boil two or three minutes. Return to colander and drain. Put in saucepan with milk or cream and butter and cook till tender. Generally no more cooking is required.

C. Shultz', Drugs and Fine Perfumery.

ESCALLOPED SALSIFY, OR VEGETABLE OYSTER.

Scrape the roots and throw them in water to prevent discoloring; cut in pieces one-fourth of an inch thick, boil till tender, remove from the water, then fill the pudding dish with a layer of the oyster plant, and a layer of crackers, rolled not too fine; salt and pepper to taste, and a plentiful supply of butter and milk enough to thoroughly moisten the quantity. Bake one hour.

Ask your grocer for Welsh's Maple Syrup.

HOW TO MAKE SALADS.

Buy suitable materials. We keep everything in Groceries, and make a specialty of Pure Goods.

202 East Broadway,
Monmouth, Illinois.
SCOTT BROS. & CO.

A WORD TO THE LADIES.

See to it that your MEN FOLKS always buy their Hats and Furnishing Goods of us.

Style—always the latest! Quality—the best! Price—just right!

Yours Truly,

J. A. HANNA & CO.,
Hatters and Men's Furnishers.

The Woman's Exchange

Is the housekeepers' best friend. Everything is prepared by Monmouth's best cooks, and therefore is just as it should be. Delicious home-made Bread, Cakes, Pies, Meats, Salads, etc. Fancy Work on hand and orders taken.

220 East Broadway.
Monmouth, Illinois.

Ida Thompson, Prop'r.

FOR FINE LAUNDRY WORK, GO TO

The Monmouth Steam Laundry Co.,

108 West First Avenue, Monmouth, Ill.

SALADS.

"The imaginary relish is so sweet that it enchants my sense."
—Troilus and Cressida.

ALMOND SALAD.
M. B.

Two-thirds celery to one-third chopped blanched almonds and mayonnaise.

APPLE SALAD.

Cut the celery as for chicken salad. Peel the apples, cut them as fine as the celery, and cover with lemon juice to keep them from turning dark. For a small family use two apples and mix with them half as much celery as you have chopped apples. Cover with a French dressing and serve on lettuce leaves if you can get them. For a company luncheon put the salad in lemon skins, lay them on lettuce, and garnish with a little mayonnaise.

COLD SLAW.
Mrs. J. H. Wallace.

Two-thirds of a cup of vinegar, one egg, two tablespoons sugar, one teaspoon salt, half teaspoon of mixed mustard, and butter size of an egg. Stir until it boils. When cold pour over the shaved cabbage. This dressing is good for any kind of salad.

HAM SALAD.

Boil ham tender and chop fine, then add tomato catsup, a little mustard and vinegar. Mix thoroughly and place in a mold.

Use Maple City Soap.

CREAM DRESSING FOR COLD SLAW.
Mary Patterson.

Two tablespoons whipped sweet cream, two of sugar and four of vinegar. Beat well and pour over cabbage, previously cut very fine and seasoned with salt.

CHICKEN SALAD.
Mrs. J. W. Sipher.

Boil with chicken one pound of loin of veal until tender. Let stand till cool, then cut with a knife in small pieces. Be careful not to use the skin of the chicken or any of the gristle. Take equal parts of meat and celery, add juice of one lemon, one-half pound English walnuts chopped. Season with salt, pepper and mix with mayonnaise dressing. Just before serving add one-half cup of whipped cream.

CHICKEN SALAD.
Mrs. Maggie Rugg.

Put one pint of vinegar and one cup of butter on stove to heat, but not to boil. Yolks of eight eggs, well beaten, with two tablespoons of mustard and one of salt. Stir these slowly into the hot vinegar and butter, and continue stirring until well cooked. Set is a cool place. It should be pretty thick, and will keep, if on ice, a long time. Cut the meat as fine as you like (not chop) from two chickens. Sprinkle with a little salt and set away in a cool place. Add about as much cut celery as meat and when ready to serve, pour on the dressing, stirring it well through, and one quart of good whipped cream. Whip part of the cream if preferred.

Ask your grocer for "Blue Ribbon" canned goods, and Olives.

FRUIT SALAD.
Harriet Gettemy Morgan.

Box of gelatine, soak in one pint of water, three lemons, one pint of boiling water, one quart of sugar, six oranges, one can of grated pineapple or sliced pineapple chopped, twelve bananas, cut in slices, or California grapes cut and the seeds taken out.

FRUIT SALAD.
B.

To one package of gelatine use one quart of boiling water. Add the juice of three or four lemons and sweeten to taste. Let the jelly become cold, then stir into it small pieces of oranges, pineapple and bananas, then set the jelly on the ice to cool and harden. This salad is improved by adding cocoanut or nut meats. Use any kind of fruit.

OYSTER SALAD.
Mrs. Jno. Clark.

Boil about twenty oysters in their own liquor five minutes. Drain. Wash in cold water then dry and place on ice. Mix with a half cup of mayonnaise, and serve on crisp lettuce leaves.

OYSTER SALAD.
Mrs. J. M. McClung.

One large can or two small cans of cove oysters. Six hard-boiled eggs, four cucumber pickles, not too large, and a little celery. Chop the whites of the eggs, pickles and celery quite fine. Chop or cut up the oysters, not too fine. Take the yolks of the eggs and mix with butter about the size of an egg and beat to a cream. Season with salt and pepper. Mix all together and thin it with vinegar to taste.

C. Shultz' Drugs and Fine Perfumery.

NUT SALAD.
Emma A. Tucker.

Take two cups of lightly chopped meats of black walnuts, English walnuts, or hickory nuts. Add two cups chopped celery, and amalgamate with sufficient quantity of very good salad dressing.

CHICKEN SALAD.
Mrs. Eliza Smith.

Yolks of eight eggs, eight tablespoons of melted butter, two teaspoons of salt, two of sugar, two of made mustard, two-thirds of a pint of vinegar. Put vinegar on stove to boil. Add the above ingredients and stir until thickens. Add more vinegar if too thick. Set off to cool. Boil chicken until tender. Take out all the bone and cut up in small pieces. Use half as much celery or cabbage as chicken. If cabbage is used add celery seed and pour dressing over, and stir lightly. Before serving add one pint of whipped cream. This will serve twenty persons.

POTATO SALAD.
Mrs. John E. Brewer.

Yolks of eight eggs, eight tablespoons of vinegar, eight tablespoons of melted butter, one teaspoon French mustard, two teaspoons sugar, three teaspooos salt, one-fourth cayenne pepper. Boil yolks of eggs. Heat the vinegar and pour hot over the beaten yolks, stirring all the time. Put back on stove and cook slowly. When done put in melted butter and mix thoroughly and add last, eight boiled potatoes, and about half as much celery, one-quarter of a pound of English walnuts, broken up. Thin down with whipped cream when ready to use.

Maple City Soaps are the best.

NASTURTIUM SALAD.
Ella Hoyt.

Line a salad bowl with nasturtium leaves. Take fully ripe tomatoes scald and slice. Cold boiled potatoes cut in dice. Onions sliced very thin. Put in salad bowl in alternate layers, pouring over all mayonnaise dressing. Chop some nasturtium seed and leaves and mix through salad.

VEAL SALAD.
Gussie Cumming.

Four pounds of veal. Three stalks of celery, two eggs, one cup of vinegar, one cup of sour cream, two spoons of sugar, one tablespoon of celery seed, one tablespoon of prepared mustard, one tablespoon of butter, one teaspoon of salt. Boil to a thick cream, and when cold, or just before serving, pour over veal and celery, chopped fine.

LOBSTER SALAD.

Make as salmon salad, using lobsters instead of salmon.

SWEETBREAD SALAD.

Use recipe for chicken or veal salad. Substituting sweetbreads, prepared by soaking in salted water two hours. Skim. Put in hot water and boil thirty minutes. Put in cold water and remove the rest of the skim.

SHRIMP SALAD.

In making shrimp salad, by adding a little cold stewed celery root (chopped) and some chopped sweet parsley and chives, the salad is remarked by every one as being so much better than the usual shrimp salad.

C. Shultz' for anything in the Drug line.

SALAD DRESSING.
Mrs. C. A. Willits.

Yolks of four eggs, one-half teaspoon mustard, one-half teaspoon salt. one teaspoon sugar. Beat thoroughly. Heat two tablespoons vinegar and two of water, add to above. Cook over hot water till it thickens. While hot beat in half as much olive oil or butter, and reduce with cream.

SALAD DRESSING.
Mrs. Jos. Stevenson.

Four eggs, one cup of vinegar, one-half pint of melted butter, two tablespoons mustard, a pinch of red pepper. Salt to taste. Beat the eggs. Mix other ingredients with melted butter, then add eggs. Boil until thick. Stir in a cup of whipped cream. Stir constantly until done.

SALAD DRESSING.
Emma Gregg.

Yolks of six eggs, well beaten, three tablespoons of oil, one teaspoon of mustard. one cup vinegar. Heat the vinegar and add to the eggs, oil and mustard. Then boil until it thickens. This makes enough dressing for two medium or large chickens.

MAYONNAISE DRESSING.

Add the well beaten yolks of five eggs to five tablespoons vinegar. Cook in double kettle until stiff, being careful to stir clean from the sides of the bowl while cooking. Remove from the fire. Add two tablespoons butter, and stir until cool and perfectly smooth. When cool, season to taste with salt, pepper, mustard, and thin with sour cream to the required consistency. With cabbage salad use sugar instead of mustard.

Ask your grocer for Anderson's Jams and Mincemeat

SALADS.

MAYONNAISE.

Rub well together one teaspoon of made mustard and one half teaspoon of salt, add the yolk of one raw egg. Pour on, very slowly, oil or melted butter, beating hard all the time until as much is made as wanted, then add a tablespoon of vinegar. The mixture should look perfectly smooth.

A nice way to eat lettuce is with lemon juice and powdered sugar, serving the lemons as for raw oysters.

POTATO SALAD.
Mrs. Wildermuth.

Six large potatoes, one large onion, whites of three hard boiled eggs, chop all together. Dressing: Yolks of three hard boiled eggs, yolk of one raw egg, half cup of vinegar, half teaspoonful of ground mustard, half teaspoonful of celery seed. Salt and pepper to taste.

PECAN SALAD.
Mrs. W. A. Hoyt.

Cut celery as for salad and mix with pecan meats, pouring over all some mayonaise dressing. Nice to serve with meats.

CHEAP POTATO SALAD.
Mrs. Peter Burns.

Chop two good sized onions very fine, chop or dice six medium sized potatoes; season with salt, add pepper and celery seed if desired. For dressing, beat two eggs and half cup of sugar together, then add one cup vinegar, put into a skillet in which butter the size of a walnut has been melted, let it come to a boil; pour over the potato and onion mixture.

Ask your grocer for "Blue Ribbon" Canned Goods and Olives.

SALADS.

POTATO SALAD.
Mrs. Jos. Stevenson.

Boil six or eight medium sized potatoes; when cold cut in small bits, with one stalk of celery cut fine; six hard boiled eggs mashed fine; a small slice of onion cut fine; pepper, salt and one tablespoon of sugar.

Dressing—Five eggs beat light; add one cup of sour cream, half cup vinegar, butter the size of a walnut; one teaspoon of mustard, a little pepper and salt, one teaspoon of sugar. Beat all well together; put on the stove and stir constantly until it comes to a boil; beat until cold and then pour over the salad.

Put in a cool place or on ice. Before serving stir in one cup of whipped cream, and serve on lettuce or cabbage leaves.

SALMON-SALAD EGGS.
Mrs. A. H. Dean.

Boil the number of eggs you desire until hard. Mix the powdered yolks with canned salmon, season with vinegar, mustard, salt and pepper. Place the mixture within the whites of the eggs and throw over them drawn butter. Serve hot.

SALMON SALAD.
Mrs. C. D. Tourtellotte.

To one can of salmon take one-fourth of a head of cabbage and two bunches of celery. Chop cabbage and celery very fine, mix it with the salmon, then add one teaspoon mustard, two-thirds cup vinegar, with one teaspoon Worcestershire sauce. Pepper and salt to taste.

SHRIMP SALAD.
M. B. S.

Eggs two, sugar four teaspoons, cream three quarters cup, vinegar three quarters cup, mustard

Ask your grocer for Welsh's Maple Syrup.

one teaspoon. salt and pepper, (a little). Boil the eggs hard; rub the yolks fine; add mustard, then the sugar, then the salt and pepper, then the vinegar slowly, and last the cream. Put into the dish in which it is to be served a layer of shrimp broken moderately fine, then a layer of celery cut fine; pour over this three or four spoons of the dressing; so continue till all is used.

TOMATO SALAD WITH SHRIMPS.

Take six large, smooth tomatoes, skin them. put upon the ice to chill, remove the inside of the tomatoes, cut it up with a silver knife into small pieces, and drain off juice, then add shrimps to this mixture, allowing four or five for each tomato, a little pepper and salt, and any good mayonnaise dressing, stir all lightly and fill the tomato shells, place again upon ice, when ready to serve put each tomato upon a lettuce leaf and add one teaspoon of mayonnaise upon the top of the mixture, which ought to be piled rather high. The success of this salad depends upon the coldness.

TONGUE SALAD.
M

Chill meat, half cup of ham, one cup tongue, one cup celery or cucumber, fourth cup chipped olives, one teaspoon salt, a little white pepper, a little lemon juice, and a little stock. Line bowl with lettuce or parsley; use mayonnaise dressing.

VEAL SALAD.
Mrs. N. S. Woodward.

Four and a half pounds veal, one bunch of celery, three boiled eggs.

Dressing: Three eggs or yolks of four or five, two tablespoons sugar, four tablespoons vinegar, one teaspoon mustard. Boil until thick as cream and let get cold.

Use Maple City Soaps.

MAYONAISE DRESSING.
Mary C. McNitt.

Yolks of two eggs well beaten (or one whole egg). one level teaspoon salt, one level teaspoon pepper, two level teaspoons sugar. two level teaspoons prepared mustard. one tablespoon of butter. Stir into this four tablespoons vinegar. Put the dressing in a bowl set in boiling water, stirring constantly until thick. This dressing is nice on sliced tomatoes.

VEGETABLE SALAD.
Mrs. W. G. Miller.

Two heads of crisp lettuce, two cucumbers, several fresh tomatoes. one small onion. a little celery. Shred the lettuce, chop the onion and celery fine, and slice the cucumbers and tomatoes. Arrange in layers on dish and pour over it any good salad dressing.

Maple City Soaps are the best.

The R. A. Wilson Company.

Books and Stationery.

Carpets, Wall Paper and Furniture.

MONMOUTH, ILLINOIS.

A GOOD RECEIPT:

Subscribe for the...... **Democrat**, and read it all the year.

—◇—

PUBLISHED EVERY THURSDAY AT $1.50 A YEAR.

—◇—

Job Printing Neatly Executed.   Quinby Block.

Have you seen the new .... ALUMINUM WARE AT SCHUSSLER'S?

Looks like silver, is light, will not tarnish, and CHEAP.

Tableware, Cooking Utensils, Spoons, etc.

Also solid Silver and Plated Ware at Greatly Reduced Prices   Bread Knives, Cake Knives, Meat Knives, Scissors, etc., etc.

| John W. Byers. | John G. Moore. | J. E. (Dick) Byers. |
| U. S. Yards, Chicago. | U. S. Yards, Chicago. | St'k Y'ds, So. Omaha, Neb. |

BYERS, MOORE & BYERS,

Live Stock Commission Merchants,

Byers Brothers & Co., | Room 109 Exchange Building. **CHICAGO.**
Stock Yards, | Union Stock Yards. . . . .
South Omaha, Neb. |

Address all communications Exchange Building, Union Stock Yards.

CHEESE.

"The queen of curds and cream."—*Winter's Tale.*

CHEESE OMELET.
Mrs. A. H. Dean.

Three-fourths of a cup of grated cheese, one cup of rolled cracker, one cup of sweet milk, two eggs, beaten separately, salt.

WELSH RAREBITS.
Mrs. T. H. Hanna

Melt slowly in a crock or porcelain kettle, rich cream cheese. Add a little cayenne. Toast bread. Butter slightly. Arrange on a plate. Pour cheese over and serve very hot.

CHEESE STRAWS.

Three tablespoons of flour, three tablespoons of Parmesan cheese, one tablespoon of butter, one tablespoon of milk, one-half saltspoon of salt, one-fourth saltspoon of pepper, one egg, yolk only. Mix the dry ingredients, and add the milk, the yolk of the egg, and the butter, softened. Mix all well with a spoon, and when smooth divide the dough in two parts. Roll these very thin, cut in narrow strips three inches long. Bake in a slow oven fifteen minutes. They may be served hot or cold. Pile on a plate in log cabin style.

CHEESE SOUFFLE.
Mrs. I. P. Pillsbury.

Two tablespoons butter, one heaping tablespoon flour. Mix together. Add yolks of three eggs,

Get a new Stove from Pinkerton & Evans.

one-half cup sweet milk, one cup grated cheese, one-half teaspoon salt, a few grains cayenne pepper. Put on stove and cook. Whip whites of eggs stiff. Mix thoroughly and turn into a buttered dish. Bake until done, about fifteen or twenty minutes, and serve immediately.

CHEESE STICKS.
Mrs. R. H. Scott.

One quart flour, one teaspoon salt, shortening as for rich paste, one and a half pints grated cheese. Mix flour and shortening, then add the cheese. Mix with milk to a stiff dough. Roll to the thickness of nearly half an inch. Sprinkle over it a little salt. Cut in narrow strips and bake to a light brown. Let them be thoroughly done before taking out.

WELSH RAREBIT.

One-half pound cheese, two eggs, one tablespoon mustard, one-half teaspoon salt, one-half cup cream, pinch of cayenne pepper. Break cheese into small bits, put the ingredients in a pan over hot water. Stir until cheese melts. Spead over toast and serve.

CHEESE FONDA.

Soak one cup dry bread crumbs in two scant cups rich milk. Beat into this three eggs whipped very light. Add one small teaspoon melted butter, one small teaspoon pepper, one small teaspoon salt, one-half pound of old cheese grated. Pour into a buttered baking dish, strew the top with dry bread crumbs, and bake a delicate brown in quick oven. Serve immediately in the baking dish, as it soon falls. This is a delicious relish.

Fresh Butter and Eggs at W. J. Patterson's.

CHEESE.

SOMETHING FOR LUNCH.

Break a quarter of a pound of cheese into bits and pound with it to a smooth paste two spoonfuls of butter, the yolks of two eggs, one teaspoon of mustard, a very little cayenne, and a half-teaspoon of salt. Toast six slices of bread, and after spreading them with the mixture, lay them in a pan in a hot oven for five minutes. Serve at once.

CHEESE STRAWS.

Grate three tablespoons any kind of cheese. Add three tablespoons flour, a little red pepper and salt. Add to the dry ingredients one tablespoon melted butter, one tablespoon water and yolk of one egg. Roll thin, as for cookies. Cut in strips. Bake fifteen minutes, or to a light brown. Delicious with salads.

CHEESE STRAWS.
Helen Dean.

One cup grated cheese, two cups flour, two tablespoons butter, (heaping). Enough cold water to thin. Pinch of cayenne. Mix butter and cheese together, add water, then flour. Roll thin. Cut in strips and bake in rather hot oven.

CHEESE CRACKERS.
M. B. S.

Place a quantity of buttered Saratoga flakes or soda crackers in a baking pan. Heaping teaspoon of rich grated cheese. Dust a little cayenne pepper over, and bake about five minutes in hot oven. Bake a light brown. Excellent with salads.

Waseca White Rose Flour at W. J. Patterson's

UNEQUALED IN QUALITY AND PRICE.

CHICAGO YEAST POWDER

Can Always be Depended Upon for

WHEN **PERFECT RESULTS ONLY HIGHEST GRADE BAKING POWDER** IS REQUIRED.

IT MAKES THE LIGHTEST BREAD:

THOSE WHO TRY IT, ALWAYS USE IT.

SOLD EVERYWHERE BY FIRST-CLASS GROCERS AT THE UNIFORM PRICE OF 25Cts PER POUND.

MANUFACTURED AND GUARANTEED BY

CHAPMAN & SMITH COMPANY,
CHICAGO.

HAWKEYE GRUB and STUMP MACHINE.

Works on either STANDING TIMBER or STUMPS. Will pull an ordinary Grub in 1½ Minutes

MAKES A CLEAN SWEEP

of two Acres at a sitting. A man, a boy and a horse can operate it. No heavy Chains or rods to handle. The crop on a few acres the first year will pay for the Machine. It will only cost you a postal card to send for an Illustrated Catalogue, giving price, terms and testimonials. Address the Manufacturers.
JAMES MILNE & SON.

Sunnyside Shetland Pony Farm

Monmouth, Illinois.

Milne Bros.,
Proprietors.

Breeders of Pure Shetland Ponies

A stock of these Beautiful and Intelligent Little Pets for children kept constantly on hand and for sale. Correspondence solicited.

Write for our pony catalogue to

MILNE BROS.,
Monmouth, Ill.

BREAD.

"Nature has meal and bran."—*Cymbeline.*

A cook can not acquire a more valuable accomplishment than that of making good bread. Nothing but experience will secure the name merited by so few—"an excellent bread maker." The first requisite is good flour; the second, good yeast; the third, watchful care. There is force in the old lament, "My bread took cold last night," too much heat carries forward the process too rapidly and the dough will become sour. Correct this by dissolving a little soda in warm water and working it in well. The oven should not be too hot. If you can not hold your bare arm in it while you count thirty, it is too quick. Keep the heat steady after the bread goes in. The time for baking is not less than three-quarters of an hour, and bread baked an hour is more wholesome.

YEAST.
Mrs. Seth Pratt.

Three pints of water, six large potatoes. When potatoes are done take the potato water and pour over one pint of flour, then add one tablespoon of salt. Mash the potatoes thoroughly and mix with the flour, and thin with cold water until cold enough to put in the yeast. Use two and one-half cakes of Magic yeast.

BREAD.
Mrs. Geo. Babcock.

At noon, boil one large potato in enough water to scald one cup of flour, when cool enough add

Ask your grocer for Epicure, N. Y. Cheese.

one-half cake of dry yeast dissolved. At night add 1 quart of warm water and make a sponge, beating well ; in the morning add one-half cup of sugar, one-half cup of melted lard and salt, and mix till smooth. Let rise, knead down, let rise again, then make into loaves, let rise and bake. To save out three or four tablespoons of the scalded yeast, before making sponge, is better for the next baking than using fresh yeast.

BREAD.
Mrs. Seth Pratt.

One pint of yeast, two pints of warm water, one tablespoon of lard, two tablespoons of sugar, mix into dough, let it rise, mould, let rise again and then mould to put into the tins.

BREAD.
Mrs. W. S. Walker.

Two quarts of flour, one cup of granulated sugar, one cup of butter, half cup of lard, one tablespoon of salt, one yeast cake dissolved in half cup of warm water, one pint of warm water; rub thoroughly together flour, sugar, butter, lard and salt, then add yeast and warm water, mould into one large loaf, let rise over night then mould into loaves, let rise until light, then bake. This will make three good sized loaves.

BREAD.
Mrs. R. A. Wilson.
(For inexperienced housekeepers.)

Save the water in which your potatoes for the noon meal were cooked. In the evening take three pints lukewarm potato water, one tablespoon sugar, one tablespoon lard, one teaspoon salt, put this into a crock and stir in nine cups of flour and two-thirds cup of home-made yeast, or its equivalent in dry

Milne Bros.—Stump Puller.

yeast. (Ordinarily this amount of flour is *right*, although some flour will do better with a *little* less.) Set this crock of sponge in flour in your bread pan, cover and set in a warm place until morning. Then use the warm flour and mix into a stiff dough, make it stiff enough so you will not need to add more flour to knead well afterward ; set in a warm place until light, then knead thoroughly once and set to rise again, when light divide into four equal parts and make four loaves, or three loaves and one pan of rolls; set in a warm place to rise, when light, bake in a moderate oven three-quarters of an hour. Divide the recipe for small baking.

BAKING POWDER BISCUIT.
Mrs. J. C. Dunbar.

Sift one quart of flour with two and a half teaspoons of Chapman & Smith's Chicago Yeast Powder, one teaspoon salt, and two teaspoons of white sugar, mix all thoroughly with the flour, sifting several times together, rub in one level tablespoon of butter, wet with half a pint of sweet milk, handle lightly and cut out with biscuit cutter, about an inch thick, and bake in quick oven 15 minutes. Water may be used instead of milk if more butter is added. Handle as little and make as rapidly as possible.

CREAM BISCUIT.
B. S.

Sift together two or three times one quart of flour and two heaping teaspoons of Chapman & Smith's Chicago Yeast Powder, work in one tablespoon of butter or lard, and half a tablespoon of salt, add one teacup of cream, and beat to a soft dough, roll to the thickness of three-fourths of an inch, cut out and bake immediately.

Sinclair Meat Co., Peoria, Breakfast Bacon.

BREAD.

DIXIE BISCUIT.
S.

Three pints of flour, two eggs, two tablespoons of lard, one cake compressed yeast, one cup milk, mix at 11 o'clock roll out at 4 o'clock, and cut with two sizes of cutters, putting the small ones on top, let rise until supper, bake twenty minutes.

MUFFINS.

Dissolve one cake of compressed yeast in a cup of warm milk, add one-half teaspoon salt, one quart of lukewarm milk, one cup sugar, one tablespoon butter, two eggs, and flour to make batter stiff enough to drop, mix at night, bake in muffin rings. Makes three dozen.

BUNS.

One pint of milk, one-half cake compressed yeast, one quart of flour—stir this well, let it rise for three hours, then add half cup of butter, rubbed to a cream with one cup of powdered sugar and one well beaten egg, add flour to make a soft dough; knead briskly; let rise until very light, then make dough into buns, quite small; set them close together on tins and let them rise; when all of a sponge, brush the tops with a little milk and sugar mixed; bake in a quick oven fifteen or twenty minutes.

SALLY LUNN.

One pint potato sponge, one-half cup milk, one teaspoon salt, one large cooking spoon butter, yolks of two eggs; mix butter and sugar together, add yolks, salt and milk, mix well, and add sponge with flour enough to make a stiff dough. If wanted for tea, set at 11 a. m., let rise untll 1 o'clock, knead again, adding flour until it does not stick to

Sinclair Meat Co., Peoria, Pure Lard.

the board, let rise until 4 o'clock, roll out in two sheets, butter one and lay the other on top, cut out with biscuit cutter, let rise, and bake in a quick oven.

SPLIT ROLLS.

One-half pint boiling milk, one pint potato sponge, one tablespoon lard aud one of sugar, one teaspoon of salt. Put one quart of flour in a bowl and add to it sugar, salt and lard, mix thoroughly and let cool, then add potato sponge and beat well. Set in a warm place to rise. When light, work in flour until it does not stick. Let rise again, roll out, butter, and cut out with biscuit cutter, double over and pinch together. Do not let them touch in the pan. Let rise again and bake in a quick oven.

CHICAGO YEAST POWDER IS GUARANTEED HIGHEST QUALITY, AND COSTS LESS THAN ANY OTHER.

REAL SCOTCH SHORT BREAD.

Two pounds of flour, one pound of butter, one-half pound of sugar ; mix to a smooth paste, half an inch thick when rolled, pinch edges, prick the top with a fork, cut in small squares, invert dripping pan, cover with paper, put cakes on and bake in a slow oven.

NEW ENGLAND BROWN BREAD.
Mrs. N. C Burlingim.

Two cups corn meal, one cup flour, two-thirds cup Orleans molasses, one teaspoon soda, one teaspoon salt, tablespoon lard or butter, one pint warm water (not scalding.) Put the meal in a dish with the molasses and salt, add the warm water, mixing thoroughly, Set in a warm place over night. In the morning add the soda dissolved in one-eighth cup of hot water. one teaspoon of baking powder in the flour. Steam six hours.

STEAMED GRAHAM BREAD.
Mrs. I. L. Moses.

One quart of sour milk, one of molasses, one of Graham flour, one of white flour, one of corn meal, one teaspoon of salt and one of soda. This makes six loaves, using quart moulds. Fill moulds half full, cover and steam three hours, remove to the oven and brown lightly.

CORN BREAD.
M. A. Kinkead.

One pint of sour milk, one of meal, one of flour, two eggs, one teaspoon soda in a little milk, one tablespoon lard, one of butter, two tablespoons of sugar, one teaspoon of salt. Stir thoroughly. Bake in a hot oven.

CORN BREAD.
Mabel Pillsbury.

One cup corn meal, one-half cup of flour, one egg, one cup sour milk, two tablespoons of sweet cream or piece of butter, two tablespoons sugar, and one-half teaspoon soda.

STEAMED BROWN BREAD.
J. M. Holt.

One cup corn meal, two cups Graham flour, one cup molasses, half teaspoon of salt, one teaspoon of soda, sour milk to make batter like cake. Steam two or three hours, and brown in the oven fifteen minutes.

SOFT CORN BREAD.
Mrs. Wm. H. Rankin.

Half pint corn meal, half pint sour milk, half pint sweet milk, tablespoon melted butter, pinch of salt, two well beaten eggs. Bake in a deep dish.

Ask your grocer for Penn Yan "1st prize" Buckwheat Flour.

FEDERAL BREAD.
Belle F. Rankin.

Two eggs, two tablespoons of butter, two tablespoons of sugar, one teaspoon salt, one teacup of sweet cream, one teacup yeast, and flour enough for a soft dough. When risen light, roll out in layers about a quarter of an inch thick, placing two in each pie pan (this quantity will make three pans full); let them rise again and bake. When done, butter between the layers, cut in pie shaped pieces, and serve hot.

CORN BREAD.
Mrs. A. H. Dean.

One cup of sugar, two eggs, one cup of sweet milk, three teaspoons baking powder, three-fourths cup corn meal, one pint flour.

SALT RISING BREAD.
Mrs. San DeLong.

Scald one heaping tablespoon corn meal with two tablespoons of new milk. Let rise over night. In the morning take two-thirds of cup new milk, one cup hot water, one-half teaspoon soda, flour enough to make sponge. Add corn meal, stir well, put in warm place to rise. When very light add one cup milk, one quart hot water, one teaspoon salt. Put all together, knead thoroughly, but not as stiff as for yeast bread. Place in pans. When light bake in moderate oven one-half hour. Care should be taken not to use too hot water. Bread must be kept warm until ready for oven.

AN EASY WAY TO MAKE BREAD.
Mrs. E. C. Johnson.

Dissolve one cake of compressed yeast in three pints of warm water, add a little salt, then stir flour in gradually until it is too stiff to work with.

Ask your grocer for Genessee Table Salt.

a spoon, then use hands, kneading it and adding flour until it is a stiff dough; use spoon to stir the flour in as long as possible; knead thoroughly for half an hour. Let rise over night in a warm place, then in the morning make into loaves, let rise one hour, bake one hour. This will make about five loaves. Bread made this way is out of the oven by 9 o'clock in the summer time.

COLD WATER BISCUIT.
Belle F. Rankin.

One quart of flour, two tablespoons lard, one teaspoon salt, mix up with enough cold water to make a stiff dough, beat it with a hatchet until it blisters, then roll into little balls, (as for rolls,) flatten with a rolling pin, stick with a fork, and bake in a hot oven until a light brown (about fifteen or twenty minutes.) This quantity makes about thirty-two biscuits.

EASY AND SURE WAY TO MAKE GOOD BREAD.
Mrs. Mira L. Miller.

First make the following yeast, which will make from twenty-four to thirty loaves of bread, and will keep two or three weeks in a cool cellar in the summer: Pare and boil six large potatoes, when done add enough water to make three pints with which scald one pint of flour, stir in mashed potatoes, add tablespoon of salt and water to make as thin as batter cakes—have warm as you can hold your hand in—add two cakes of Yeast Foam which have been soaked in lukewarm water several hours; keep in warm place until fermentation ceases—about ten or twelve hours.

To make bread.—In the morning put one quart of water, as hot as you can bear your hand in, into flour, add one tablespoon of lard, two scant

See Morrell & Co's ad. on page 48.

tablespoons sugar, and one-half teaspoon salt, and one pint of the yeast; knead well and put in warm place, when light knead again, when light, again, make in four loaves and put in pans. Your bread should be baked before noon in winter, earlier in summer. A two gallon jar heated and greased is the best to put bread in to raise.

OCEAN GROVE CORN BREAD.
Mrs. Duke.

One cup of butter, four eggs, three tablespoons sugar, half teaspoon of salt, four teaspoons of baking powder, one pint sweet milk, one pint of corn meal and one quart flour.

GERMAN WAFFLES.
Mrs. H. Warner.

One-half pound butter beat to a cream, then add the yolks of twelve eggs, sugar enough to sweeten to your taste. Stir this like pound cake, then add one cup of milk, some blanched ground almonds, and a teaspoon of almond flavoring, one teaspoon baking powder, and enough flour to make it stiff as pancake batter; last of all add the whites of the eggs well beaten. Bake in waffle irons, and sprinkle with sugar before sending to table.

Montgomery—Dry Goods.

PIES AND PUDDINGS.

"Allow not nature more than nature needs."—*King Lear*.

PUFF PASTE.

Take equal quantities of flour and butter. before mixing wash the butter thoroughly, then lay in ice water. take the flour, adding a teaspoonful of salt for each pound of flour, mix into a stiff. smooth paste, using ice water for mixing, allow the dough to lie five minutes, after which roll large enough to work in butter, fold twice so it will be four thicknesses, repeat five times, leaving the paste about ten minutes each time. then work paste in desired form, a cool place is desirable for making paste.

PIE CRUST.

Three cups of flour to one of lard makes three pies. Rub lard lightly in flour; salt. Pour in enough ice water to roll out; mix lightly with a knife. For lemon, chocolate and all pies of that character, bake the crust first. prick lightly with a fork to prevent blistering, then add the custard. already prepared by cooking in double boiler. This is much better than where the custard is baked in the pie.

GOOD PIE CRUST.

A quart of flour will make four pies. Sift the flour with a teaspoon of baking powder; rub in a quarter of a pound of lard or butter, then moisten with ice water, using as little as will make the flour stick together. Do not work it with warm hands.

Wright & Graham Artistic Tailors.

PIES AND PUDDINGS.

APPLE PIE.

Peel and slice three apples, put in the crust; pour on a half teacup of water, a teacup of sugar mixed with a tablespoon of flour; a small piece of butter and nutmeg grated.

APPLE CUSTARD PIE.

One pint of sour apples cooked smooth and sifted, two cups of sugar, one cup of butter, six eggs beaten separately; the whites for frosting the top; season with mace and cinnamon. This makes five pies.

BLACKBERRY PIE.

One pint of berries, one teacup of sugar mixed with a tablespoon of flour to prevent the juice from boiling out; water if necessary.

CHESS PIE.
Julia Clark.

Three eggs, two-thirds cup sugar, half cup butter, half cup mlik. Beat butter to a cream, add yolks and sugar beaten to a froth, with one teaspoon vanilla. Stir together rapidly and bake in a nice crust. When done spread with the beaten whites of the eggs and three tablespoons of sugar. Return to oven and brown slightly.

CREAM PIE.
Miss Minnie Babcock.

One pint cream, one tablespoon corn starch mixed smooth in a little of the cream, sugar to taste, vanilla; whites of two eggs well beaten added to mixture when just ready for oven. Bake slowly and serve very cold.

CREAM PIE.
Ruth Ray.

Lay in a pie plate a crust as for custard pie. Stir to a cream half a cup of sugar and one table-

Genuine N. O. Molasses at W. J. Patterson's.

spoon butter. Add the yellow of two eggs, two tablespoons flour and two cups of milk. Mix all together and flavor with lemon. When done beat the whites of two eggs with two tablespoons of sugar. Spread over pie. Return to oven to brown.

CREAM PIE.
Mrs. Henry Ewing.

One cup of sugar, three tablespoons of flour, three eggs, butter size of an egg, one and a half teacup new milk, one and a half teacup new cream, flour, with lemon or vanilla extract. This receipt makes two pies.

CREAM PIE.
Mrs. Ida Weir.

One egg, half cup cream, half cup milk, half cup sugar, nutmeg to taste, one tablespoon corn starch; let the milk and cream come to the boil, then add the egg, sugar and corn starch; then place in baked crust and frost.

CREAM PIE.
Sadie Neville.

One and one-half cups powdered sugar, one tablespoon flour, a little grated nutmeg, one pint cream. Stir together. Beat the whites of three eggs to a stiff froth. Add this to the cream, beating well. Bake in a slow oven. This makes enough filling for two pies.

CREAM PIE.
Mrs. T. H. Hanna.

Take four eggs (leaving out the whites of two), one cup sugar, half cup flour, a little salt; mix these smooth with a little cold milk and stir into one quart of boiling milk; simmer slowly until thick, stirring all the time; flavor with vanilla or lemon; pour this into newly baked crust and bake

"*They call for dates and quinces in the pastry.*"
—*Romeo and Juliet.*

five minutes. Beat the two whites of eggs to a stiff froth, add half cup of sugar; spread over top and brown lightly.

COCOANUT PIE.
Mrs. W. B. Wolf.

Whites [Yolks] of four eggs, one cup cocoanut (prepared), one cup sugar, one quart new milk, pinch of salt, four tablespoons flour. Put milk on stove, let come to a boil; add cocoanut and sugar; mix flour thoroughly with cold milk, then add to boiling milk; lastly the eggs well beaten. Stir gently. Bake the crust before putting the mixture in. Beat the whites of four eggs, add eight teaspoons pulverized sugar, vanilla flavoring; spread over the top and sprinkle with cocoanut; place in oven and brown delicately. This makes two pies.

"ROLLING-PIN" CLEANED CURRANTS ARE READY FOR INSTANT USE. NO WASHING OR CLEANING REQUIRED.

COCOANUT PIE.
Mrs. Ida Weir.

One pint milk, half cup sugar, half cup cocoanut, one tablespoon butter, two tablespoons flour; cook until thick, then add whites of two eggs and pour into the crust, which has been previously baked. Frost with whites of two eggs and place in oven to brown.

COCOANUT PIE.
Mrs. Eliza B. Smith.

One cup of sweet milk, half cup of cocoanut, whites of two eggs, half cup of sugar, one tablespoon of butter, flour enough to thicken. Put the milk, cocoanut and butter in a dish placed in another one filled with water to boil. Rub flour and sugar together with a little milk and add to boiling milk. When thick add the whites of eggs beaten. Set aside to cool. Make a rich puff paste; when this is cool, pour in the filling. Spread over the pie the whites of two eggs, well beaten.

Sprinkle half cup cocoanut and two tablespoons of sugar over the top. Place in oven to brown.

COCOANUT CREAM PIE.
Mrs. H. F. Eaton.

One pint milk, one cup sugar. one tablespoon butter. four tablespoons flour. whites four eggs. one cup prepared cocoanut. pinch of salt. Scald the pint of milk over steam; add sugar. cocoanut and butter. then the flour and salt which have been mixed with cold milk. and lastly the beaten whites of eggs: stir gently. Bake crust after pricking with a fork. When both are cold spread the mixture over crust. Then beat whites of four eggs. add eight teaspoons pulverized sugar; spread this over top and lastly sprinkle one-fourth cup cocoanut over top. and brown lightly. This makes two pies. If fresh cocoanut is used half of one is enough. It will then be necessary to use a little sugar with that sprinkled over top.

CHOCOLATE PIE.
Mrs. W. J McQuiston.

Yolks of three eggs. two large tablespoons grated chocolate, one teaspoon of flour, two-thirds cup of sugar. one cup of sweet milk, a very little butter; set on the stove till it thickens; flavor with vanilla; bake with an under crust: beat the whites, add two teaspoons of sugar: spread on the pie and brown slightly. Serve cold.

LEMON PIE.
Mrs. R. A. Wilson.

One lemon, one cup sugar, one coffee cup water, yolks of two eggs, two very heaping tablespoons of flour. Mix the flour and sugar together and add the beaten yolks of the eggs and the juice of the lemon with a very little of the grated rind, then add the cup of cold water. Put this into a

---

"Wishers were ever fools."—Anthony and Cleopatra.

rice boiler and cook until it looks clear and thick; put into the crust which has been baked. Make a meringue with the whites of the eggs, one or two tablespoons of sugar and a little vanilla, and put on the top of the pie and brown slightly in the oven.

LEMON PIE.
Mrs. Henry H. Pattee and Mrs. J. Shultz.

One cup sugar, one cup water, one lemon, one tablespoon corn starch, two eggs (leaving white of one for the meringue). Boil sugar and water until dissolved, add juice and grated rind of lemon, beaten eggs and corn starch mixed smooth with little cold water; cook until it thickens; do not scorch; pour into a pan lined with rich paste and previously baked; return to the oven and bake until firm; beat white of egg stiff, add tablespoon sugar, spread over top and set in the oven for a few minutes.

LEMON PIE.
J. Ida Parrot.

Three lemons, three spoons butter, four eggs, one cup sugar. Grate rinds and use juice. Melt butter. Stir all together and bake with under crust. Frost with whites of four eggs, sweetening with four tablespoons sugar. Brown delicately. Sufficient for two pies.

LEMON PIE.
Mrs. Eliza B. Smith.

One teacup of water, the grated rind and juice of one lemon, one cup sugar, yellow of two eggs, two tablespoons of flour, butter size of walnut. Put water in double boiler, and place on stove. Add one-half sugar to water. Beat the eggs with the other half cup sugar. Add butter and lemon, then thicken with the flour. Let boil fifteen min-

"Ill blows the wind that profits nobody."—Henry IV.

utes, stirring all the time. Have crust baked. Pour in filling when cool. Beat whites of two eggs and spread over top, and sprinkle with two tablespoons of sugar. Place in oven to brown.

TWO CRUST LEMON PIE.
Mrs. M. L. Dougherty.

Three lemons for two pies. Two cups of boiling water, two tablespoons of corn starch, one cup of sugar. three eggs.

LEMON CUSTARD PIE.
Mrs. D. Turnbull.

Two lemons grated, two coffee cups boiling water, two and one-half tablespoons corn starch. two coffee cups sugar. yolks of three eggs. Put the corn starch, sugar and water on the fire and let it remain until it becomes thick, stirring constantly, then pour it on the eggs and lemons. Will make three small pies or two large ones.

MINCE MEAT.
Ida Armsby.

Four pounds meat, one and one-half pounds of suet. As much apple as both suet and meat, three pounds raisins, one pound citron, one and one-half pounds figs, two nutmegs, ten cts. of cinnamon, five cts. cloves, one teaspoon of pepper, four pints of New Orleans molasses, four pints C sugar, juice of two lemons, one cup of vinegar, two and one-half quarts boiled cider, two tablespoons salt. Boil one hour.

MINCE MEAT.
Mrs. H. M. Graham.

Three bowls chopped meat, five of chopped apples, five of brown sugar, one of shredded suet, two of seeded raisins, one of Orleans molasses, one of

---

"To whom God will, there be the victory."
—Henry VI.

PIES AND PUDDINGS. 93

vinegar, one of fruit syrup or jelly, one of cider, one of chopped citron, three tablespoons cinnamon, two tablespoons cloves, one tablespoon salt, one tablespoon pepper, five nutmegs, grated. Mix all together. Put in granite kettle. Set on the stove, heat through thoroughly, then set away for use. For measurement use pint bowl.

TOMATO MINCE FOR PIES.
Mrs. Sarah Ruse.

One peck of green tomatoes. Five pounds of sugar, two pounds of raisins, one tablespoon of cloves, one tablespoon cinnamon, one tablespoon allspice, one tablespoon nutmeg. Chop the tomatoes fine and cook one hour and a half, then add the sugar and spice, with one lemon and half a cup of vinegar, and the raisins chopped fine. Use a teaspoon of salt and half a one of pepper, and cook half an hour. This will keep in an open jar all winter. Delicious.

MOCK MINCE PIE.
Mrs. San DeLong.

Six soda crackers rolled fine, one cup molasses, one cup hot water, half cup sugar, half cup vinegar, half cup melted butter, one cup chopped raisins, one teaspoon each of cloves, cinnamon, allspice and nutmeg. Measure in coffee cup. The above will make four pies.

MOCK MINCE PIE.

For two large pies. Four crackers, one cup molasses, one cup sugar, two-thirds cup butter or chopped salt pork, two eggs, one teaspoon each of cloves and cinnamon, one cup chopped raisins.

Exercise, sun and air will give good appetite and sound sleep.

ORANGE PIE.
Mrs. Jennie Hawley.

One orange, one small cup sugar, one small cup sweet milk, two eggs, one tablespoon flour, one teaspoon butter. Grate the orange and mix with sugar, butter, yolks of eggs and flour; beat thoroughly, add milk, and bake with one crust. Beat the white of the eggs to a stiff froth, add sugar to make quite sweet, and when the pie is done, spread the frosting smoothly on top, return to oven and let remain until a light brown. Try this once and you will try it again.

THE MOST DELICATE FLAVORS ARE OBTAINED FROM **CHICAGO FLAVORING EXTRACTS.**

PUMPKIN PIE.
M. B. S.

Select deep yellow pumpkin, fine grained. Pare and cook slowly. When soft, and the water all boiled off, mash and set back on the stove where it can simmer until the pumpkin becomes brown and waxy. Put through a colander, and to scant three pints of the pumpkin add eight well-beaten eggs, one teaspoon mace, one teaspoon cinnamon, one teaspoon ginger, half a nutmeg, a little salt, two cups light brown sugar, and two quarts of good sweet milk. Bake slowly until a nice golden brown. Prepare the pumpkin the day before.

PUMPKIN PIE.
Mrs. W A. Robison.

In preparing the pumpkin, cook from six to eight hours. To one pint of pumpkin take two eggs, one cup granulated sugar, one-half saltspoon salt, the same of pepper, one tablespoon butter, one-half nutmeg, one teaspoon ginger, one pint good sweet milk. Delicious.

PINEAPPLE PIE.
M. B. S.

Use either fresh or canned pineapples, grated. Sweeten to taste. Small piece of butter. Bake with one crust, with strips over top.

PINEAPPLE PIE.
Mrs. Chas. Collins.

One cup sugar, one-half cup butter, one cup sweet cream, five eggs, one pineapple grated. Beat the butter and sugar to a cream. Add the beaten yolks of eggs, the pineapple and cream, and lastly the beaten whites, whipped in lightly. Bake with under crust.

RHUBARB PIE.
Ruth Ray.

Pour boiling water over two teacups of chopped rhubarb. Drain off the water after four or five minutes, and mix with the rhubarb one teacup of sugar, the yolk of an egg, a piece of butter the size of walnut, a tablespoon of flour. Moistening the whole with three tablespoons of water. Bake with a lower crust only. When done beat the whites of two eggs and two tablespoons of sugar. Spread over top and return to oven.

SQUASH PIE
Mrs. H. Burlingim.

Squash one large pint, sugar two cups, milk one' quart, butter two tablespoons, cracker three tablespoons, eggs four, ginger one teaspoon, extract of lemon one teaspoon, salt one teaspoon. Peel the squash, steam it soft, and strain it. To a large pint, add sugar, spice, salt and cracker crumbs, the latter rolled fine. Boil the milk, and melt the butter in it. Pour this gradually over the squash,

"In a false quarrel there is no true valour."
—*Much Ado About Nothing.*

stirring all the time. When thoroughly mixed add the eggs well beaten. Bake in deep plates, with a nice under crust. Excellent.

WASHINGTON PIE.
Mrs. F. P. Gilbert.

One cup sugar, one egg, half cup sweet milk, one heaping tablespoon butter, one and a half cups flour, one heaping teaspoon Chapman & Smith's Chicago Yeast Powder, nutmeg to taste. Bake in two layers in quick oven. Filling—Into one pint of boiling milk stir the following: One tablespoon corn starch dissolved in a little milk, yolks of two eggs, half cup sugar. After this is cooked thoroughly, beat the whites of the eggs to a stiff froth and stir into the cream while cream is still hot. Flavor with lemon. Spread between layers of cake and serve fresh. This makes a very nice dinner dessert.

PUDDINGS.

APPLE PUDDING.
Mrs. J. Shultz.

Fill a buttered baking dish with sliced apples, and pour over the top a batter made of one tablespoon of butter, half cup of sugar, one egg, half cup sweet milk, and one cup of flour in which has been sifted one teaspoon baking powder. Bake in a moderate oven. Serve with sugar and cream. Use peaches the same way.

APPLE DUMPLINGS.
Mrs J. B. Herbert.

Pare, core and quarter good cooking apples; have ready well buttered cups; take one pint flour,

"He that is proud, eats up himself."
—*Troilus and Cressida.*

two teaspoons of baking powder, a little salt, and sufficient milk to make a thick batter; put in each cup a spoonful of batter, add prepared apples, cover with batter, and steam until fruit is thoroughly cooked. Serve with sugar and cream.

APPLE TAPIOCA.
Mrs. Geo. Babcock.

Soak one cup tapioca in one quart water over night pare and slice a dish of apples, adding a little water and sugar. Bake. When nearly done, pour tapioca over apples and return to oven. Cook until it jellies. Eat with cream and sugar.

A DELICATE DESSERT.
Mrs. Mary Pillsbury.

Bake a sponge cake. Have it two inches deep when done. Over this pour boiled custard. Just before serving slice some peaches and put over the cake. Beat the whites of the eggs to a froth and put over the top. For custard use the yolks of the eggs and whites for the top. Oranges may be used instead of peaches.

BOILED APPLE PUDDING.
Mrs. Sarah K. Miller.

Pare and core six apples, put them in a stew pan with water enough to half cover them, add one teacup of sugar and butter the size of an egg, a pinch of salt; boil until the underside of the apple is tender, then turn them over, thicken with a tablespoon of flour mixed in cold water; essence to suit.

BREAD PUDDING
Mrs. J R Hickman.

One pint bread crumbs, one cup molasses, one of raisins (seeded), one of water, one of flour, one egg, one teaspoon of soda; steam two hours.

Use Maple City Toilet Soaps.

BANANAS IN SYRUP
Mrs. Jas. French.

Heat in a porcelain kettle a pint of currant and red raspberry juice, equal parts, sweetened to taste. When boiling, drop into it a dozen peeled bananas; simmer them very gently for twenty minutes; remove the bananas, boil the juice until thickened to the consistency of syrup, pour over the fruit. Serve cold.

BANANA SNOW.
Mrs. Eliza Smith.

Soak two-thirds box of gelatine in one-half cup of cold water for half an hour, then pour over this one pint of boiling water, add a heaping cup of sugar, juice of two lemons, stir well, when cold and beginning to thicken add whites of three well beaten eggs; beat all together until stiff and white (about one hour.) Peel, cut in thin slices eight large bananas and stir into the snow. Dip molds into cold water, fill with the snow, set on ice to harden. Serve with whipped cream or custard made of the yolks of eggs, one pint milk and half cup sugar.

BAKED APPLES.
Mrs. Mary A. Frantz.

Cut apples in halves, take out cores, set in baking pan with the cored side up. For seven or eight tart apples use 3 cups sugar, $1\frac{1}{2}$ cups water, set on top of stove, cover closely and let boil half an hour, remove cover and place in oven, an bake until brown as desired.

CURRANT PUDDING.
Mrs. Fred Patterson

One egg, two tablespoons sugar, one tablespoon butter, three-fourths cup sweet milk, one cup of

---

"*Good words are better than bad strokes.*"
—*Julius Cæsar.*

currants, two tablespoons baking powder, a little salt. Put in enough flour to make it a stiff batter. Steam half an hour. Serve hot. Sauce for pudding—Beat one egg until light, then add three-fourths cup of sugar, one cup of sweet milk, one tablespoon butter. Place this on the stove, let it stand until hot, then remove from stove and flavor with vanilla extract.

COTTAGE PUDDING.
Mrs. Draper Babcock.

One cup sugar, one of sweet milk, one egg, two tablespoons butter, two teaspoons Chapman & Smith's Chicago yeast powder, two cups flour, steam two and one-half hours.

Sauce for same.—One pint water in a basin, three tablespoons sugar and a little salt, one tablespoon butter, and let it boil ten minutes, then add thickening—flour and water mixed very smooth. Strain the same if there are any lumps of flour, it should be about as thick as cream. Flavor with lemon or vanilla.

CHOCOLATE PUDDING.

One quart milk in which scald nine tablespoons grated bread crumbs and five tablespoons chocolate. Then take from the fire and add the beaten yolks of four eggs, sweeten to the taste, and season with vanilla. Bake one-half hour. Then put the whites, well beaten, over the top, with two tablespoons of sugar, and let stand in the oven until a light brown.

COCOANUT AND CORN STARCH BLANC MANGE
Mrs Jas French.

Simmer two tablespoons of prepared cocoanut in a pint of milk for twenty minutes and strain

Chapman & Smith's Extracts are delicious in Pies.

through a fine sieve. If necessary, add more cold milk to make a full pint. Add a tablespoon of sugar, heat to boiling, and stir in gradually two tablespoons of corn starch, rub smooth in a very little cold milk; cook five minutes, turn into cups and serve cold with fruit sauce or cream.

DIPLOMATIC PUDDING.
Hannah Tilson.

Dissolve one box of gelatine in one cup of cold water, (it will take about one hour.) For lemon syrup use one cup of water, half cup lemon juice, two cups sugar—warm until sugar is melted. For orange sponge, use one cup of orange juice, two cups of sugar, whites of three eggs beaten, and one-fourth teaspoon cream tartar, Divide the gelatine about equal parts. Pour the syrup into one-half gelatine and the sponge in the other half. Mould the syrup placing in a large mould, stand a smaller mould in the middle of it, fill the small mould with cold water until the syrup is solid, then remove the small mould and fill the cavity with sponge and let cool.

IN-EVERY RECIPE WHERE BAKING POWDER IS REQUIRED USE **CHICAGO YEAST POWDER.**

DANDY PUDDING.
Mrs. H. P. Smith.

One quart milk, four eggs, two tablespoons corn starch, half cup sugar, one teaspoon vanilla ; put the milk on to boil ; moisten the corn starch with a little cold milk, and add to the boiling milk; stir and boil five minutes; beat the yolks of the eggs and sugar together until light, and add to the boiling milk; take from the fire, add the flavoring, and pour into a baking dish; beat the whites of the eggs to a very stiff froth, add to them two tablespoons powdered sugar, and heap on the top of the pudding; put it in the oven for a few minutes until a light brown. Serve ice cold.

DAINTY PUDDING.
E. Tucker, Chicago, Ill.

Take two ounces of citron, and one orange. Grate two large cups of stale bread, and soften it with a cupful of water. Grate the rind and squeeze the juice of the orange, cut the citron in small bits and mix them with the bread, together with the yolks of two or three eggs, and sugar enough to sweeten the mixture. Butter six small cups. Just before putting the pudding in the oven, beat the whites of the eggs to a stiff froth, quickly mix them with the bread and fruit, distribute them in the buttered cups and bake the little puddings slowly for about twenty minutes, or until they are brown. They are to be served hot and with cream sauce.

DELMONICO.
Mrs. Lizzie Shultz.

Yolks of six eggs beaten very light ; then add one coffee cup of granulated sugar, one-third of a vanilla bean steeped in half pint cream. (Do not boil.) One-half box Cox's gelatine in half teacup warm water, stir until thoroughly dissolved ; then add the warm cream to the gelatine and stir the eggs and sugar into this; whip one quart of rich cream, and stir into the other ingredients. Freezer should be all prepared first, as gelatine is apt to congeal if not frozen quickly. This quantity will make one gallon.

ENGLISH PLUM PUDDING.
Mrs. J. Shultz.

One pound each of finely chopped suet, sugar, currants, stoned raisins, two pounds soaked bread,

Never borrow if you can possibly avoid it.

six well beaten eggs, one teaspoon of salt, two teaspoons of baking powder, one grated nutmeg; mix all together thoroughly; take a square piece of cotton cloth, dip it in scalding hot water, flour it well and lay it over a pan, place the pudding in the cloth and tie it closely: put it in a pot of boiling water for five hours. Have boiling hot water ready to fill the pot as it boils away, so as not to let it get below boiling heat.

Sauce:—One cup of sugar, half cup of butter beat to a cream, a teacup of boiling water, two teaspoons of flour scalded together: flavor to suit taste.

ENGLISH PLUM PUDDING.
Mrs. E. I. Camm.

One pound suet (shredded and chopped fine), one pound bread crumbs, one pound sugar, one pound raisins (seeded), one pound currants, one-fourth pound citron, one-fourth pound candied lemon peel, one pint milk, eight eggs, three tablespoons cinnamon, two tablespoons cloves, one tablespoon mace, one nutmeg, one teaspoon soda. Put in a well buttered mould and steam eight hours. Serve with hard sauce.

Hard sauce:—Two cups sugar, one-half cup butter beaten to a cream, yolks of two eggs; flavor with lemon.

FRUIT SALAD.
Mrs. Eliza Smith.

One box gelatine, pour over it one pint of cold water, soak one hour, add three cups of sugar, juice and grated rind of four lemons. Stir in three pints of boiling water—if cool weather four pints—then strain and add fruit, while jelly is warm, six oranges, six bananas, one can of sliced or grated pine apple. Set aside to cool. This will serve forty people.

Sunshine is one of nature's most potent remedies.

FRENCH PUDDING
Mrs. Henry Ewing.

Beat four eggs very light. Make a batter of two teacups of flour, three teacups of milk, and one of cream, pour in the eggs and beat all well together, Add a tablespoon of melted butter and bake from twenty to thirty minutes. Serve with white sauce.

FRUIT PUDDING.
Mrs. T. H. Davidson.

One cup milk, one egg, piece of butter size of an egg, one teaspoon soda, two small teaspoons cream of tartar, flour to make a stiff batter, one cup of tart fruit. Steam one hour. Serve with any rich sauce preferred.

FIG PUDDING.
Mary R. Irwin.

Six ounces of figs, chopped fine, six ounce of suet, three ounces of bread crumbs, three ounces of sugar, three eggs, and a little nutmeg. Steam three hours. Sauce—Beat up one teacup of butter to a cream as for cake, add two cups of sugar, and flavor with a teaspoon of vanilla.

FIG PUDDING.
Mrs. Geo. Wiley, Chicago.

One cup sweetening (one-half sugar and one-half N. O. molasses,) half cup butter (scant,) one cup sweet milk, two eggs, three and one-half cups flour, two heaping teaspoons baking powder, one pound figs chopped very fine.

Sauce for Fig Pudding.—Two tablespoons of boiling water poured over two tablespoons butter. Beat in with Dover egg beater, two cups powdered sugar; flavor with juice of a lemon.

The happiness of your life depends much upon the character of your thoughts.

GRAHAM PUDDING.
Mrs. O. D. Hawkins.

One cup molasses, one of sweet milk, one of raisins, two of Graham flour, two teaspoons soda, and a little salt. Stir the molasses and milk, divide the flour and stir in raisins, then soda in part of flour, stir all together. Put in round cake tin with a pipe in, and steam two and one-half hours. Have ready cup of powdered sugar, scant half cup butter beaten to a cream, moulded into a brick, set out to cool on a plate. Then cut your pudding like cake and cut a slice of the cream, and serve on plate with the pudding.

GROUND ALMOND PUDDING BOILED.
Mrs. H. Warner.

One-half pound ground almonds, one-half pound white sifted sugar, eight eggs, beaten separately, one-half pound of bread crumbs. The rind of a grated lemon. Beat for half an hour and steam the same as for other steamed puddings. Must be dished up quickly and eaten with sauce.

INDIAN PUDDING.

To one quart of milk, when hot, add four tablespoons of corn meal thick enough to make porridge. When cool add half cup chopped suet, two eggs, with sugar to taste, salt, cinnamon and nutmeg. Bake two hours.

INDIAN PUDDING.
Mrs. H. Burlingim.

Boil two quarts of milk; salt. While boiling stir in one and one-half cups corn meal. While hot add one cup of suet, one cup of molasses, one tablespoon of cinnamon, one teaspoon of ginger. Let cool; add three well beaten eggs, piece of butter half the size of an egg, one cup of raisins, one of

The cheapest foods are oatmeal, beans and potatoes.

Chapman & Smith's cleaned currants, and sugar enough to serve without sauce if you wish. Sauce the same as for English plum pudding, which makes it delicious. Bake three hours slowly.

MOONSHINE PUDDING.
Mrs. Edna Brown.

Whites of six eggs, beaten stiff. Add gradually six tablespoons of powdered sugar, beating for not less than fifteen minutes. Then put in one tablespoon preserved peaches in small bits. In each saucer put in some rich cream, whipped, sweetened and flavored with vanilla, and on the cream place a liberal portion of the moonshine. This makes enough for eight persons.

NESSELRODE PUDDING.
Mrs. Eliza Smith.

One pint almonds blanched, and one pint chestnuts blanched, and pounded into a paste, one pint cream, one pint pineapple, ten yolks of eggs, one-half pound candied fruit, one tablespoon of vanilla, one pint water, one pint sugar. Boil sugar, water and pineapple juice twenty minutes. Beat yolks and stir into this. Put the pan in which this mixture is into boiling water, beat until it thickens. Place in a pan of cold water, beat ten minutes, mix with cream, rub through a scive. Add fruit and pineapple, cut fine. Mix all together. Add one-half teaspoon salt, vanilla. Freeze like ice cream.

ORANGE PUDDING.
Mrs. C C. Merrideth.

Five oranges cut up and laid nicely in a dish with one coffee cup of sugar poured over them. Let one pint of rich milk get boiling hot; stir in the yolks of three eggs and one tablespoon of corn

"Man is a giddy thing. and this is my conclusion."
—*Much Ado About Nothing.*

starch; when thick pour over the oranges. Beat the whites with one tablespoon of sugar; spread over the pudding and brown in the oven. Serve cold.

PRUNE PUDDING.
Ella Rogers.

To one quart prunes add one quart water and sugar to taste. Cook slowly until quite soft. It will require several hours. Pour off syrup, seed the prunes and put them in a baking dish with the syrup and the beaten whites of six eggs mixed in. Bake fifteen or twenty minutes in a moderate oven. Serve with whipped cream.

PEACH CREAM.

Pare and stone some nice yellow peaches and mash through a colander with a potato masher. Allow as much cream as peach pulp, sweeten to taste and beat until the cream is light. Serve in glasses with currant buns. Banana cream may be made in same way.

PUDDING.
Mrs. Wilber S. Walker.

One-half cup of butter, one and a half cup of sugar, two-thirds cup of milk, the whites of four eggs, three cups of sifted flour, three teaspoons of baking powder, one teaspoon each of vanilla and lemon extract. Sauce for pudding—Beat one egg until light, add juice of two lemons, half cup of sugar. Boil all together until thick.

PUDDING SAUCE.
Margaret Owens.

One cup sugar, one-half cup butter, yolks two eggs. Beat all together very light, then add the whites well beaten. Flavor to taste. Steam over boiling water.

Press not a falling man too far.

RICE PUDDING.
Mrs. Sarah Miller.

One cup of rice soaked over night in a cup of cold water. When time to cook add one cup of raisins, one cup of sugar, one piece of butter, one nutmeg, nine cups of milk. Bake one hour.

SCOTCH PIE.

Slice four or five tart apples in a granite pie pan. Add two tablespoons water. Cover with a mixture made like biscuits, using either sour milk and soda, or sweet milk and baking powder, only a little more shortening. Stir with a spoon stiff enough to spread over apples. Serve with apples up, and cover plentifully with a sauce made of one tablespoon flour, butter size of an egg, three-fourths cup of sugar, nutmeg. Stir with a little cold water. Pour over one pint of boiling water. Boil five minutes or till clear. A simple and good dessert. Good cold or warmed over.

STEAMED PUDDING.
Mrs. I. H. Wolfe.

One cup sugar, two-thirds cup butter, one cup sweet milk, one cup raisins, three cups flour, one teaspoon soda, one teaspoon all kinds spices. Steam two hours. Serve hot with a dressing of ten tablespoons of powdered sugar, two tablespoons of butter, whip to a cream. Add the whites of two eggs beaten stiff. Season with vanilla.

STEAMED PUDDING.
Mrs. L. M. Daugherty.

One and one-half cups of sugar, one cup sweet milk, three cups flour, one-half cup butter, one egg,

"My salad days—when I was green in judgment."
—*Antony and Cleopatra.*

one good teaspoon of soda, one teaspoon of cinnamon, one teaspoon of cloves, one-half cup of chopped citron, one cup of raisins or currants. Sauce for pudding—One-half cup of butter, one-half cup flour, one cup of sugar. Mix thoroughly. Add one pint of boiling water. Stir briskly and cook fifteen minutes.

SUET PUDDING.
Mrs. Alice Carey.

Two-thirds cup of suet, chopped fine. One cup of sugar, one egg, one teaspoon cinnamon, two teaspoons of baking powder, one-half cup of water, one cup of raisins, two cups of flour. Steam two hours. Sauce for the above—Two cups sugar, one tablespoon corn starch, one pint boiling water. one teaspoon butter. Boil five minutes. Flavor with lemon.

THE MOST DELICATE FLAVORS ARE OBTAINED FROM **CHICAGO FLAVORING EXTRACT**

SUET PUDDING.
Alice Winbigler.

Two cups bread crumbs, one cup raisins, one-half cup suet, one cup sweet milk, one teaspoon soda, one teaspoon cinnamon, one-half teaspoon cloves, one tablespoon sugar, pinch of salt. Steam two hours. Pudding sauce—Six tablespoons sugar, two tablespoons butter, one of flour, teaspoon nutmeg. Mix well together and add ten tablespoons boiling water. Cook until done.

SUET PUDDING.
Mrs. Edgar MacDill.

One cup chopped suet, one cup molasses, one pint fruit, one cup sweet milk, one teaspoon soda, mixed in molasses, four cups flour. Spice to taste. Steam three hours. Any kind of sauce.

SAUCE FOR BREAD PUDDING.
Mrs. E. C. Johnson.

One tablespoon of flour, one tablespoon of butter, two tablespoons of sugar, one tablespoon vinegar, one cup of sweet milk, two cups of boiling hot water, stirred in gradually. Boil briskly for about three minutes.

SUET PUDDING.
Mrs. Duke.

One cup of suet, one cup of molasses, one cup sour milk, one cup of chopped raisins, two cups of flour, one teaspoon soda. Flavor with nutmeg and cloves. Steam three hours.

STRAWBERRY SHORTCAKE.

One and one-half cups flour, three tablespoons butter, three teaspoons baking powder; make soft dough like biscuit; moisten with milk or water; bake in two layers. One quart or more strawberries, sweeten to taste and partly mash; butter layers and put berries between.

STEAMED PUDDING.
Mrs. Henry H. Pattee.

One and one-half cups fine bread crumbs, one-half cup flour, one teaspoon cream tartar mixed with it; three-fourths cup chopped suet, three-fourths cup stoned raisins, one-half cup molasses, one-half cup milk, one-half teaspoon soda dissolved with the molasses, one-half teaspoon salt, one-half teaspoon cloves. one-half teaspoon cinnamon, nutmeg to taste. Steam three hours. Serve hot.

Sauce:—One teacup sugar, one half cup water, one cup milk, one teaspoon butter, one teaspoon corn starch dissolved in a little milk. Boil till well done. Pour this over the white of one egg beaten stiff.

"Striving to do better, oft we mar what's well."
—*King Lear.*

SNOW CUSTARD.
Sara Bond-Hanley.

Half package gelatine, three eggs, one-half cups of sugar, juice of one lemon. Soak gelatine one hour in cup of cold water. then add sugar, lemon juice, and one pint boiling water; stir until dissolved, and set away till quite cold; then beat the whites of eggs very stiff and whip the gelatine in them spoonful at a time, whipping slowly and evenly for half an hour or till quite stiff. Serve in sherbet cups with whipped cream piled on top. Or can be moulded in small cups and served with plain custard made of the yolks of the eggs.

SAGO PUDDING.
Mrs. Janie S. Pebbles.

To three pints boiling water add one cup of sago. Boil until the sago is transparent, then add one cup sugar; let cook a few minutes then add four tablespoons sour jelly (currant is best), stir until dissolved; take from the fire and add one teaspoon vanilla. Pour into a dish you wish to serve it from and when cold eat with sweetened cream flavored with vanilla.

STEAM PUDDING WITHOUT EGGS.
Mrs. W. E. Burns.

One quart flour, one pound chopped raisins, one and one-half cup chopped suet, one teacup molasses, one teacup brown sugar, one teaspoon soda, two cups sweet milk, little salt. Steam four hours.

TRANSPARENT PUDDING.
Mrs. Henry J. Ewing.

Yolks of eight eggs, three-fourths pound butter, one pound sugar, one nutmeg, one pint cream; mix well, put into a pan and set over a vessel of boiling water for a few minutes. To be baked in rich puff paste.

Life is a shuttle.

TRIFLES.

One quart flour, one cup sugar, two tablespoons melted butter, a little salt, two teaspoons baking powder, one egg, sweet milk sufficient to make rather stiff. Roll out in thin sheets, cut in pieces about two by four inches; make as many cuts across the short way as possible, inserting the knife near one edge and ending the cutting just before reaching the other. Pass two knitting needles under every other strip, spread the needles as far apart as possible, and with them hold the trifles in the fat until a light brown. Only one can be fried at a time.

TAPIOCA WITH PINEAPPLE.
Mrs. J. P. Stevenson, Tarkio, Mo.

One-half cup tapioca. Soak over night in enough water to cover. In the morning add two pints of water and cook slowly until transparent. One and one-half cups of sugar and a little salt. Bake one hour. Remove and add one-half can of grated pineapple. Serve with whipped cream.

TAYLOR PUDDING.
Mrs. Lucy Clark.

One cup of molasses, one cup of suet, one cup of sweet milk, one teaspoon soda, flour to thicken, raisins or currants. Steam two hours. Sauce— One egg, tablespoon flour, one-half cup of sugar, one spoon of butter. Mix and thicken with boiling water.

THE QUEEN OF PUDDINGS.
Mrs. E. B. Doolittle.

Take one pint of nice bread crumbs, add a quart of milk and one cup of sugar, the yolks of four eggs well beaten, and the rind of a fresh

Moore hated onions. He said that a man who would eat onions would steal.

lemon grated, a piece of butter the size of an egg, one spoon of flour and bake well. Beat the whites of the eggs to a stiff froth and add one cup of pulverized sugar and the juice of the lemon. Spread over the pudding a layer of jelly and then the whites of the eggs and bake a light brown.

TAPIOCA PUDDING.
Mrs. I. M. Matthews.

Cover three tablespoons of tapioca with water and soak over night. In the morning drain and add one quart milk and one small cup of sugar and boil half an hour. Then add the yolks of four eggs and boil five minutes. Beat the whites and spread on top and brown in the oven.

WOODFORD PUDDING.
Mrs. Eli Dixson, Roseville; Mrs. C. M. Johnson.

Three eggs, one cup sugar, one-half cup butter, three-fourths cup flour, one teaspoon soda dissolved in one-third cup sour milk. one teacup jam (raspberry). Bake slowly.

Sauce for above: Three eggs (the yolks), one cup sugar, butter the size of an egg; cream, butter and sugar together. Make thin as desired with boiling water. Put in a bowl and set in a vessel of hot water. Use whites of the eggs for top of pudding.

LEMON SAUCE FOR PUDDINGS.
Mrs. A. B. Seaman.

Two cups hot water, one cup sugar, three teaspoons corn starch, grated rind and juice of one lemon, one tablespoon butter. Boil the water and sugar five minutes and add the corn starch wet in a little cold water. Cook about ten minutes, then add the lemon and butter. Stir until the butter is

---

Balfe said there was nothing better than fish and potato salad.

melted and serve at once. If the water boil away and the sauce become too thick add more hot water till of the right consistency.

CORN MEAL PUDDING.
Mrs J. C. Gettemy.

Five eggs beaten separately, three tablespoons sugar, three tablespoons corn meal. Beat sugar, yolks and meal together, stir in whites lightly. Serve with hot sauce.

JELLIED PEACHES.
Mrs. Geo. Babcock.

Drain juice from a can of peaches, add one cup sugar and boil ten minutes. Add one-half box gelatine soaked in cup cold water. Take from stove as you put in gelatine. When thoroughly dissolved, strain over peaches. Eat cold with cream and sugar.

DUTCH APPLE CAKE.
Mrs. A. B. Seaman.

One pint flour, one-half teaspoonful salt, one-half teaspoonful soda sifted into the flour, one teaspoonful cream of tartar, one-fourth cup butter, one egg, one scant cup milk, four sour apples, two tablespoons sugar. Mix the dry ingredients in the order given; rub in the butter; beat the egg and mix it with the milk, then stir into the dry mixture. The dough should be soft enough to spread half an inch thick on a shallow baking pan. Core, pare and cut four or five apples into eighths; lay them in parallel rows on top of the dough, the sharp edge down and pressed slightly into it. Sprinkle the sugar on the apple, with a little cinnamon if desired. Bake in hot oven twenty or thirty minutes. Serve with lemon sauce as a pudding.

"The sands are numbered that make up my life."
—Henry VI.

ICES.

"A dream, a breath, a froth of fleeting joy."—*Poems. Shakespeare.*

APRICOT SHERBET.
Mrs. E. A. Lord.

One pint of canned apricots, rubbed through a sieve, one pint sugar, one pint milk, one pint water. Mix and freeze.

LEMON SHERBET.
Lucy Duer.

One quart new milk, one pound sugar, five lemons, three eggs. Boil the milk with the lemon rinds, add the suffar, and when cold put in freezer and partly freeze. Then add the juice of five lemons, slightly sweetened, and the whites of three eggs, beaten stiff. Freeze hard.

MILK SHERBET.

Juice of four lemons, one and a half cups sugar, one quart milk, whites of three eggs beaten to a stiff froth. Freeze and pack hard.

ORANGE SHERBET.
Mrs. Edna B. Brown.

Juice of ten oranges, one pint of sugar, two pints of water, two eggs (whites only). Freeze.

SUN SHERBET.
Georgia A. Smith, Galesburg, Ill.

Juice of four lemons, two cups of sugar, whites of four eggs. Stir sugar and lemon juice together, add the well beaten whites, beating all the time. Add the milk, still beating hard, just before pouring into the freezer.

A light heart lives long.

MRS. DEARBORN'S SHERBET.

Boil one pound of sugar and one quart of water ten minutes, Pour this over two ounces of raisins stoned and cut in small pieces; cool. Soak two teaspoons of Knox's granulated gelatine in one-fourth cup of cold water five minutes, strain. Dissolve with one-half cup of hot water. Add this to cold syrup, strain. Add one cup of fruit syrup to the strained mixture, add also the juice of three oranges and one lemon, strained. Put all in freezer, freeze to a mush. The syrup is that used in soda fountains and any desired flavor may be used.

LEMON ICE.
Mrs. E. A. Lord.

Boil one quart of water with three-fourths pound of sugar, add the juice of three lemons, strain and freeze. When partly frozen add the beaten white of one egg.

PINEAPPLE ICE.
(One gallon.)
Margaret Owens.

One can of pine apples, four lemons, whites of four eggs, one pint of sugar. Make a thick syrup of the sugar and pour over the beaten eggs as for icing, add the pineapple well chopped, then the juice of the lemons and one pint and a half of water. Add sugar to taste

PINEAPPLE ICE.
Mrs. E. A. Lord.

Three lemons, one can sliced pineapple, one and one-half pints sugar, two quarts water, one large tablespoon gelatine, whites of two eggs. Soak gelatine in a little water two hours. Boil water and sugar five minutes and set aside to cool.

Ladies, do your cooking with Galva Soft Coal, and ask for our Ice, cheapest and best—Sipher.

Chop the pineapple fine. Use it this way or strain out the juice as you like best. Mix lemon juice, syrup and gelatine, strain. Add pineapple and freeze. When nearly frozen add the beaten whites of two eggs.

ORANGE ICE.
Mrs. Eugene A. Lord.

Twelve large oranges, one pint of sugar, one quart water, one tablespoon gelatine, white of one egg. Prepare the same as for pineapple ice.

PINEAPPLE ICE.
Mrs. Edgar MacDill.

One quart water, two-thirds pint of sugar, the juice of one and one-half lemons, strain. The juice from one can of grated pineapple. When partly frozen add the beaten white of an egg. Too make more, double all the receipt except pineapple.

STRAWBERRY ICE CREAM.
Mrs. Edgar MacDill.

One quart berries, strain, one pint sugar, mashed together, one pint milk, one quart cream. Freeze.

STRAWBERRY ICE CREAM.
Mrs. O S French.

One pint of rich milk, one pint of cream, one quart of fresh strawberries mashed with one and one-half pints of sugar, one teaspoon of vanilla. Mix all together and freeze.

AMERICAN CREAM.
Mrs. C. W. Dougherty.

One quart milk. five eggs, one-half box Cox's gelatine. Soak the gelatine one-half hour in a little more cold water than will cover it well, then add the cold milk. Put over fire and stir until

---

Schubert loved corned beef and cabbage better than any other dish.

the gelatine is dissolved. Add the yolks of the eggs beaten with ten tablespoons sugar and let boil about two minutes. Beat the whites of the eggs with six tablespoons sugar. Pour the custard over the whites and beat until well mixed. Flavor with one teaspoon vanilla. Pour into a mold and set in a cold place. Should be made at least five hours before using.

BANANA CREAM.
Mrs. Delos P. Phelps.

Remove skins from five large bananas and rub them smooth with five tablespoons of white sugar, beat one-half pint of cream to a stiff froth, add the pounded fruit and a little lemon juice; mix well and add one-half ounce Cox's gelatine previously dissolved in enough rich milk to cover it; whisk all together gently and mold. Cream and sugar may be served with this.

CHARLOTTE RUSSE.
Linnie Brewer.

One pint thick cream well whipped, the whites of three eggs beaten stiff; have all ready one-fourth box of gelatine dissolved in half cup warm water. Let it cool before putting in the cream. Beat thoroughly after the gelatine is added, sweeten and flavor with Chapman & Smith's vanilla to suit the taste. This will serve ten persons.

CARAMEL ICE CREAM.
Julia Clarke.

One pint milk, two eggs, two cups sugar, one quart cream, two tablespoons flour, one tablespoon flavoring (vanilla), one saltspoon salt. Scald the milk in double boiler. Beat the eggs, flour and one cup of sugar together till light, then turn into the milk. Stir constantly till thickened and then occasionally. Cook in all twenty minutes. When

Liszt was as simple in his eating as he was abstruse in his music.

cold add the second cup of sugar. the cream and flavoring, then strain into the freezer and freeze. Put one scant cup of sugar into a frying pan and stir over the fire until the sugar turns liquid and brown, add this to the hot custard, in place of one cup of sugar.

CHOCOLATE ICE CREAM.
Mrs. Geo. Babcock.

One pint rich cream, one pint new milk, one egg, one tablespoon corn starch. one cup sugar, one and one-half tablespoons chocolate. Heat milk. adding sugar, corn starch and chocolate dissolved in a little of the milk. Beat egg and add to milk, etc., stirring constantly till thick. Set off fire and add cream. When cold add vanilla and freeze.

COFFEE CREAM.
Adelaide M. Glenn.

Make one-half pint of custard with two eggs and one-half pint of milk. Dissolve one ounce of gelatine and three tablespoons of sugar, one-half cup of strong coffee. add the custard and strain. Whip one-half pint of cream quite firm, stir lightly into the custard. When it is cool pour into a mold and set on ice. Coffee must be filtered, not boiled, freshly made and very strong; three tablespoons of coffee to the half pint.

Coffee Ice Cream may be made by not using the gelatine and freezing it in a freezer.

FROZEN PUDDING.
Mrs. L. Marks.

Two cups granulated sugar, two eggs, two tablespoons gelatine, one-half cup flour, one quart cream, one pint milk, three-fourths pounds candied fruit, one spoon vanilla. Dissolve flour in a little milk, add sugar and eggs and add the milk

"Omittance is no quittance."—As You Like It.

boiling hot. Cook in double boiler twenty minutes, then add gelatine which has soaked two hours, and set away to cool. Freeze ten minutes, then add fruit, and finish freezing.

GELATINE JELLY.
Mrs. J. F. Gainer.

A half box gelatine dissolved in one pint warm water, add one quart boiling water, two and a half cups sugar, one tablespoon citric acid dissolved in a little cold water; boil twenty minutes; flavor with banana essence. It can also be used for a salad by pouring over ripe fruit, bananas sliced, green grapes, oranges, etc. Let stand twenty-four hours on ice before using.

ORANGE CUSTARD.

Make a rich custard with the yolks of eggs, using Chapman & Smith's delicious orange extract for flavoring. Beat whites to stiff froth, and stir through custard while hot. Or, put in grated chocolate and flavor with vanilla, and you will have an excellent chocolate custard.

SWEET POTATO CUSTARD.
Mrs. Eliza B. Smith.

Rub cup of sweet potatoes through a colander; beat two eggs into the potato and add half teacup of sugar. Flavor with nutmeg or any spice. Add piece of butter the size of a hickory nut. One cup of milk. Salt to taste.

ORANGE CUSTARD.
Mrs. Ida Weir.

One quart milk, one tablespoon corn starch, five tablespoons sugar, a very small pinch of salt, six drops of vanilla, one whole egg and yolks of three (save whites of three for frosting.) Pare three oranges, cut into very small pieces, and sprinkle

Hodgens' Tutti Frutti Cream.

six or seven tablespoonsful of sugar over them, and set aside for two or three hours. Put milk into a tin pail in a kettle of hot water with the salt, keep out about one-half cup of milk to dissolve corn starch; add the well beaten eggs and cook until thick.

TAPIOCA CREAM.
Mrs. L. M. Reed.

Three tablespoons tapioca soaked over night in water to cover. Add three pints of milk, boil five minutes (using double boiler), stir in yolks of four eggs, one cup of sugar. Let scald. Add whites of four eggs beaten to a froth. Flavor with Chapman & Smith's extract of vanilla.

VELVET BLANC MANGE.
Emma A. Tucker.

Two cup sweet cream, half ounce Cooper's gelatine, soaked in very little cold water one hour, one-half cup powdered white sugar, one teaspoon Chapman & Smith's extract bitter almonds. Heat the cream to boiling, stir in the gelatine and sugar, and as soon as they are dissolved take from the fire, beat ten minutes; flavor and pour into mould wet with cold water. Stick over the top—when turned out and ready to serve—blanched almonds.

A Rubber Stamp
For Marking Your Linen, Sheets, etc.
Made to order in any style at the

MONMOUTH RUBBER STAMP WORKS,

where you can also have your menus printed in attractive shape.

CAKES.

"He that would have a cake out of the wheat, must tarry the grinding Hereafter the kneading, the making of the cakes, the heating of the oven, and the baking ; nay, you must stay the cooling, too, or you may chance to burn your lips "
—*Troilus and Cressida.*

Cake makers often condemn the recipe when the fault lies in themselves. Here are a few general rules: Always use the best materials. When commencing have all the ingredients ready, weighed or measured, the tins lined with paper and greased (or grease the pans, have them cold and dust well with flour.) For cakes which require [long baking use several layers of paper. Use granulated sugar dried and sifted. Always dry the flour and sift it four times with the baking powder into a dry dish. In making anything of the cake kind begin with the shortening and sugar, creaming them with the hand in a deep earthen bowl to a light and delicate consistency, adding the yolks of eggs, which should be beaten separately from the whites, stirring them in thoroughly with a wooden spoon ; then add milk or water gradually, beating all the time. This adding of the liquid slowly prevents curdling. Or alternate with flour a little at a time. Add flavor, then flour, and finally fold in the whites of the eggs, beaten to a coarse froth, stiff enough to cut with a knife, but never to the hard, dry froth which some patent egg beaters give. Use a fork or wire spoon for beating. In the folding process the motion with the spoon is from right to left.

"ROLLING-PIN" - CLEANED - CURRANTS.

THE PLUMPEST
CLEANEST
MEATIEST
AND FINEST FLAVORED.

They are ready for instant use, and for convenience are put up in 1 and 2 lb. cartons.

DELICIOUS! THAT'S JUST WHAT THEY ARE.

SO ARE **CHICAGO FLAVORING EXTRACTS.**

THEY ARE PURE.
THEY ARE FULL STRENGTH.
THEY HAVE THE MOST NATURAL AND DELICATE FLAVOR.
THEY ARE ABSOLUTELY UNEQUALED.
EVERY BOTTLE FULL MEASURE, AND BEARS THIS [TRADE MARK]

CHAPMAN & SMITH COMPANY,
MANUFACTURERS AND IMPORTERS,
CHICAGO, ILL.

THE FAMOUS.

Leaders in Styles and Prices of Clothing, and Gents Furnishing Goods.

LIONEL WOLFERMAN,
PROPRIETOR.

"The New Departure."

BUY THE BEST!

The New Departure

The Original and Only Genuine

Tongueless Cultivator.

None genuine unless bearing our trade mark; "The New Departure" on arch.

PATTEE PLOW CO.,
Monmouth, Ill.
Patentees and Sole Manufacturers.

ANGELFOOD CAKE.
Mrs. Eliza B. Smith.

Whites of ten eggs, one tumbler of fine granulated sugar, one tumbler of winter wheat flour, one teaspoon cream of tartar, and a little salt. Sift the sugar before measuring. Sift the flour, add cream of tartar and salt. Sift three times. Beat the whites of the eggs until light. Beat the sugar in thoroughly and add the flour. Flavor to taste. Bake one hour.

BERWICK SPONGE CAKE.
Mrs. L. A. Green.

Six eggs beat together three minutes,
Three cups sugar, beat this five minutes,
Two cups of flour,
Two teaspoons cream tartar beat two minutes,
One cup water with one small spoon soda dissolved in it ; beat one minute, a little salt and lemon extract. Bake in slow oven.

BRIDGET'S CUP CAKE.
Mrs. M. E. Babcock

Two heaping cups bread dough,
One small cup butter, Two small cups sugar,
Half teaspoon soda dissolved, Three eggs,
One cup seeded raisins,
Cloves, cinnamon and vanilla.
Let this rise until very light before baking.

COFFEE CAKE.

One cup coffee cold and strong, One cup butter,
One cup sugar, One cup molasses,
Four and one-half cups flour and two eggs,
One teaspoon of soda dissolved in water,
One teaspoon cinnamon and cloves,
One cup Chapman & Smith's currants.

C. Shultz, Pure Spices.

CAKES

BROWN STONE FRONT CAKE.
Mrs. H. Burlingim.

Half cup chocolate shaved, Half cup sweet milk,
One cup sugar, Yolk of one egg.
Boil till thickens and cool.
Three-fourths cup sugar, Two-thirds cup butter,
Two eggs, One cup milk,
Two and one-half cups flour,
Two teaspoons Chapman & Smith's Chicago Yeast Powder.
Add the chocolate. Bake in shallow, oblong tin.

COFFEE CAKE.
Mrs. Carrie L. Wallace.

One cup butter, One cup sugar,
One cup molasses, One cup coffee (liquid),
Four cups flour, Three eggs,
One teaspoon soda, Two teaspoons cloves,
Two teaspoons cinnamon, One ℔. chopped raisins,
Two teaspoons mace or one of nutmeg.

CREAM SPONGE.
Mrs. L. A. Green.

Two eggs broken in a cup and fill with sweet cream,
One cup fine sugar, One heaping cup of flour,
Two teaspoons baking powder. Flavor to suit.

MARBLE CAKE.
Mrs. F. A. Gilmore.

Whites of five eggs, One-half cup of butter,
Two cups of sugar, One cup of sweet milk,
Three cups of flour,
Two teaspoons of baking powder.

For the dark part—One cup of dough, add one cake of grated chocolate, dissolved in a little milk. Use one-half of the white dough first, then all of the dark part, the remainder of the white last.

W. J. Patterson, Groceries and School Supplies.

CAKES.

CRACKER CAKE WITHOUT FLOUR.

Ten eggs, Two cups sugar,
Two teaspoons cinnamon, Juice and rind of a lemon,
Two bars chocolate grated, Half ℔. dates cut fine,
Dredge with a little flour,
Eleven soda crackers rolled fine.
Bake in a moderate oven.

PRINCESS ALEXANDRIA CAKE.
Mrs. Lafayette Marks.

One cup sugar, Whites of four eggs whipped stiff,
One-third cup sweet milk, One-third cup butter,
Two teaspoons baking powder in $1\frac{1}{2}$ cups of flour.
Bake in an oven just hot enough to hiss lightly when touched with water. Flavor to taste.

PORK CAKE.
Mary Patterson.

One pound salt pork chopped fine,
One pound raisins, One pound currants,
One pint brown sugar, Half pound citron,
One pint boiling water, Half pint molasses,
One heaping quart flour, One teaspoon mace,
Two teaspoons each of cloves, cinnamon and nutmeg
Rind of one lemon grated,
One tablespoon soda dissolved in hot water.
Pour the boiling water on pork, stir until melted, then pass through the colander, add sugar, molasses, spices and half the flour—flour first—then add soda and rest of flour. Bake in well buttered cake pan in a hot and steady oven,

RAIL ROAD CAKE.
Mrs. Edna Brown.

Two tablespoons butter, Two cups sugar,
One cup sweet milk, Four eggs, Three cups flour,
Two teaspoons baking powder.

Genuine New Orleans Molasses at W. J. Patterson's

CAKES.

SPICE CAKE.
Mrs. Chas. M. Johnson.

One cup butter, Two cups brown sugar,
Three cups flour, Four eggs,
One cup cold coffee, One bowl of citron,
One bowl chopped raisins, One teaspoon cinnamon
One teaspoon nutmeg, Half teaspoon cloves,
One teaspoon lemon extract,
Two and one-half teaspoons baking powder.
Bake in slow oven.

SPONGE CAKE.
Miss Emma Gregg.

Five eggs, Two cups sugar,
Half cup warm water, Two cups flour.
Flavor with lemon.

SPONGE CAKE.
Mrs. L. M. Dougherty.

One cup sugar, One cup flour,
Two tablespoons water, Three eggs,
One teaspoon of baking powder,
One teaspoon of lemon.

Beat the yolks of the eggs, sugar, flour and water together, add the whites well beaten. Bake twenty minutes.

SPICE CAKE.
Mrs. Mira L. Miller.

Two cups sugar, One cup butter,
One cup strong coffee, Four cups of flour,
Three eggs,
Three scant teaspoons baking powder,
One teaspoon each of cinnamon and allspice,
One-half teaspoon cloves,
One nutmeg, One pound raisins seeded,
One-half cup citron, One-half cup figs.

"Oh what a goodly outside falsehood hath."
—*Merchant of Venice.*

SUNSHINE CAKE.
Miss Anna B. Owens.

Whites of seven eggs, Yolks of five eggs,
One cup sugar, Four-fifths cup flour,
One-third teaspoon cream of tartar.
Flavor to taste. Mix as in angel food.

FRUIT CAKE.
Mrs. J. Shultz.

One pound brown sugar, One pound flour, browned
Three pounds seeded raisins,
Two pounds Chapman & Smith's cleaned currants,
One pound figs, Three-fourths lb butter,
One cup molasses,
Two teaspoons mace, cinnamon and cloves,
One teaspoon pepper, One teaspoon nutmeg,
One teaspoon soda, One dozen eggs,
One-half cup currant jelly melted in one-half cup of hot water.
This cake will keep for years.

FRUIT CAKE.
Mrs. Seth Pratt, Roseville.

One pound flour, One pound butter,
One and one-half pounds sugar (very brown)
Four pounds raisins chopped fine.
Three pounds Chapman & Smith's currants,
One-half pound citron, chopped,
Ten eggs, One-half ounce nutmeg,
One-half ounce cloves, One-half ounce cinnamon,
One-half pint coffee.

EASILY MADE FRUIT CAKE.
Mrs. J. F. Alexander.

Two cups sugar, Three-fourth cups butter,
Three cups flour, One cup sour milk.
One teaspoon soda.

"We are born to do benefits."—Timon of Athens.

Five eggs, yolks beaten with butter and sugar, whites added last with flour,
One pint seeded raisins,
One pint Chapman & Smith's cleaned currants,
One-fourth pound citron, roll fruit in a little flour, small tablespoon cinnamon, allspice, cloves and nutmeg. Bake two hours in slow oven, cover top with paper while baking.

FRUIT CAKE.
Mrs. James Duke.

Four lbs seeded raisins chopped,
Two lbs Chapman & Smith's cleaned currants,
One lb each of citron and figs cut very fine,
One lb brown sugar,   One lb flour,
One lb butter,   One dozen eggs,
One tablespoon allspice, Two tablespoons cloves,
Two tablespoons cinnamon,
One nutmeg,   One cup molasses,
One teaspoon of soda dissolved in a gill of hot water.

Cream butter and sugar, mix flour and spices. Then beat all together adding fruit last well floured. This will make two loaves. Bake in moderate oven three hours, frosting when cold.

WHITE CAKE.
Mrs. John J. Glenn.

Two cups sugar,   One cup butter,
One cup sweet milk,   Three cups flour,
▭ Three small teaspoons baking powder.
Whites of seven eggs.

WHITE FRUIT CAKE.
S. B. M.

One heaping cup sugar, One-half cup butter,
One cup sweet milk,   Two cups flour,

"*There's not one wise man among twenty that will praise himself.*"—*Much Ado About Nothing.*

One cup chopped raisins,
One-half cup citron rolled in flour,
Whites of four eggs,
Two teaspoons baking powder.

WHITE FRUIT CAKE.
Carrie Smith.

One cup butter   Two cups sugar,
Three cups flour,   Whites of eight eggs,
One-half cup water,   One-fourth lb citron,
Two teaspoons baking powder,
One-half lb almonds chopped very fine,
One teacup cocoanut.

Cream butter and sugar, add the eggs, then the flour, lastly fruit; bake in two loaves forty minutes in a moderate oven.

VELVET SPONGE CAKE.
Mrs. Irene E. Smith.

Two cups sugar,
Six eggs, leaving out whites of three,
One cup boiling water,
Two and one-half cups flour,
One tablespoon baking powder,

Beat yolks a little, add sugar and beat fifteen minutes, add the three beaten whites and cup of boiling water just before the flour. One teaspoon lemon flavoring. Bake in three tins.

MY WEDDING CAKE 42 YEARS AGO.
Mrs. M. E. Babcock.

One pound sugar,   Yolks of eight eggs,
Three whole eggs,   One pound butter,
One and one-fourth lb. flour, Four pounds currants,
Three pounds raisins,   Half pound citron,
One cup molasses,
Two tablespoons cinnamon,

Careless measurement spoils many good dishes.

Teaspoon each of mace, cloves, vanilla and lemon. One teaspoon of soda dissolved in hot water. Work butter and sugar together until very light, also yolks of eggs; put whites in last and soda. Bake three hours with slow fire.

RAISED CAKE.
Mrs. H. Burlingim.

Two cups light bread sponge,
Two-thirds cup butter, Two cups of sugar,
One teaspoon soda, Three eggs.

Mix these ingredients well, add the sponge with flour to make as stiff as cup cake. Cinnamon, cloves and nutmeg, and Chapman & Smith's extract of spice. One cup raisins, one cup Chapman & Smith's cleaned currants, citron and figs improve it. Let raise about two hours.

HARD TIMES FRUIT CAKE.
Mrs. J. W. Matthews.

Soak one cup of dried apples over night—chop,
Add one cup molasses, Half cup of vinegar,
Let it simmer two or three hours.
Beat to a cream one egg and yolks of two more,
One cup brown sugar, One-half cup butter,
Add two and one-half cups flour.
One-half cup sweet milk,
One and one-half teaspoons soda,
Cinnamon, cloves, nutmeg, and prepared apples. Bake slowly. Use the two whites for frosting.

WHITE MOUNTAIN CAKE.
Mrs. Henry Ewing.

Two cups of butter, Three cups of sugar,
Five cups of flour, One cup of milk,
Four teaspons baking powder, Eight eggs.
Use coffee cups. Flavor to taste.

C. Shultz, Pure Spices.

DELICATE CAKE.
Mrs. Henry Ewing.

One pound of flour, One pound of sugar,
Half pound of butter, Whites of sixteen eggs.

LAYER CAKES.

ALMOND CREAM CAKE.

Whites of ten eggs.
One and a half goblets pulverized sugar.
One and a half goblets flour.
One heaping teaspoon cream tartar.

For Cream.

Half pint sweet cream. Yolks three eggs.
One tablespoon pulverized sugar.
One teaspoon corn starch dissolved in milk.

Beat eggs and sugar together; boil cream. add eggs, sugar and corn starch. Blanch and chop one and a half pounds almonds and stir in the cream. Put together like jelly cake.

PRINCE ALBERT CAKE.
J. M. Holt.

One and half cups sugar. Two eggs.
One half cup butter. Three-quarters cup milk.
Two heaping cups flour.
One and a half teaspoons baking powder.

Bake half in shallow tins. to the remainder add one tablespoon of molasses. one cup of raisins mixed with a spoonful of flour. one-half spoonful of cinnamon, cloves and nutmeg. Put together with icing flavored to taste.

FRENCH CREAM CAKE.
Dora Dougherty.

Whites of five eggs. Two cups of sugar.
One cup butter. One cup of sweet milk.
Three and a half cups of flour.
Two teaspoons of baking powder.

"What's past help should be past grief,"
—Winter's Tale.

Filling—One tablespoons of corn starch dissolved in milk, yolk of two eggs, one half cup of sugar, a small piece of butter. Have one pint of sweet milk boiling. stir in the ingredients and boil until the thickness of cream, when cool spread between the layers of the cake. Flavor with Chapman & Smith's pineapple.

CHOCOLATE CAKE.
Edna Dean.

Two cups sugar.   Half cup butter.
Half cake of chocolate, melted.
Four eggs.   One cup sweet milk.
Two teaspoons baking powder.
Two cups flour.

Mix butter and sugar to cream, add chocolate and milk and yolks of eggs. Sift baking powder with flour, and add alternately with whites of eggs. Bake in two layers.

Icing — Two cups granulated sugar, one-half cup of boiling water. flavoring extract. Boil until it hairs. and pour over the whites of two eggs, beaten stiff. Beat until thick.

SPICED FIG CAKE.
Miss Linnie Brewer.

One cup of butter.   Two cups of sugar.
One cup of milk.   Four cups flour.
Two teaspoons baking powder.

Five yolks and two whites of eggs or seven yolks, if prefered, using three whites for frosting. Flavor with fresh lemon. Work the butter soft and light, mix the sugar in slow and keep the butter light. put in part of the milk and flour. then the eggs well beaten. whites and yellows together. Bake in three pans. two of yellow, and in a third of the dough put two teaspoons cinnamon. one-half

---

"*Words without thoughts never to heaven go.*"
—*Hamlet.*

teaspoon of cloves, a little nutmeg and vanilla. Put one pound of figs, chopped in a pan on the stove with a little water and let simmer until tender, remove on a plate and dry off. When the cake is done take two-thirds of a cup of sugar to the whites of each egg, put water over the sugar, enough to dissolve and boil until thick enough to thread as it drops from a spoon. Have the whites beaten very light and drop the sugar slowly, a spoonful at a time, beat very light and put a thin layer on the cake first, then the figs and another layer of frosting; put the spiced layer between the yellow ones, leaving frosting enough to cover when all put together. This makes a large loaf.

LEMON CAKE.
Sara Peacock.

Two cups sugar. Three-fourths cup butter.
Three cups flour. One cup milk.
Whites of five egg. Two teaspoons of baking powder. Bake in jelly tins and between the layers spread the following:
One egg. One cup of sugar.
One lemon, juice and rind.
One teaspoon of butter.
Boil till thick as jelly.

LEMON CAKE.
Mrs. L. Marks.

One cup butter. Two cups sugar.
Three cups flour. One cup sweet milk.
Four eggs whipped separately.
Two teaspoons baking powder.
Filling—Dissolve two tablespoons corn starch or flour in a little water, add juice and rinds of two lemons, yolks of three eggs, one cup sugar, half cup butter and one cup boiling water. Cook in

Knowledge comes, but wisdom lingers.

double boiler, and just as removed from stove add the whites, whipped stiff.

PORK CAKE.
No eggs or butter required.
One-half pound pickled pork, chopped very fine.
One cup molasses. One cup sugar.
One teaspoon soda dissolved in a cup of boiling water. Six cups of flour. One cup each of raisins and Chapman & Smith's cleaned currants, and spice to suit the taste. Have the batter about as thick as ginger bread.

PRINCE OF WALES CAKE.
Mrs. Lafayette Marks.
One cup brown sugar. A little soda.
Two large spoons baking powder.
Two cups flour. Half pound raisins.
Half cup sour milk. A little citron.
Half cup butter. Spice to taste.
Yolks of three eggs.
Bake in layers and put together with frosting.

WHITE LAYER CAKE.
Mrs. Eliza B. Smith.
Whites of seven eggs. Two-thirds cup of butter.
Two cups granulated sugar. Beat to a cream.
One cup sweet milk. Three cups flour.
Two teaspoons baking powder. Flavor to taste.
Use this filling, or any other:

Filling—One small cup of water, one cup granulated sugar, yolks of three eggs, juice and grated rind of one lemon, two heaping tablespoons of flour. Place these ingredients on the stove in a double boiler, the egg being first well beaten. Boil till thick, letting it cook one-half hour. When cool spread on cake.

"An honest tale speeds best being plainly told."
—*Richard IV.*

STRAWBERRY JAM CAKE.
Mrs. L. S. Linn.

One-fourth cup butter. One cup sugar.
Three eggs.
Three tablespoons of sour milk.
One and two-thirds cups of flour.
One teaspoon cinnamon. One teaspoon soda.
One cup jam.
Bake in layers and put together with boiled icing.

MARSH MALLOW CAKE.
Mrs. F. B.

Make any nice white cake and bake in two long tins, boil two cups granulated sugar and one-half cup water five minutes, or until it strings from the spoon, have the whites of two eggs beaten stiff, and pour the hot syrup into them, stirring fast; while very hot stir in one box of marsh mallows; put half between the cakes and half on top.

CONSERVE.

One and one-half cups maple or white sugar, one cup sweet cream, one tablespoon butter, one teaspoon vanilla; mix and simmer gently forty minutes.

FILLING FOR LAYER CAKE.
Mrs. J. O. M.

One cup of nice cream, two tablespoons sugar, ten cents' worth English walnuts and rolled fine; any flavor you wish. This filling can be made with sour cream by using more sugar; beat the cream up, then add the sugar, nuts, etc., and put between layers and on top cake.

ALMOND FILLING.

One cup sweet cream set in a basin of hot water, heat for two or three minutes, add the yolks of three eggs, and one teaspoonful of corn starch dissolved in a little milk; sweeten to taste, cook till it

Striving to better, oft we mar what's well.

thickens, remove from the fire, add one-half cup of almonds, blanched and chopped (not too fine), when cool flavor with vanilla, cover the top of the cake with a thick frosting and sprinkle some almonds on top.

ICE CREAM FILLING.
Harriet Gettemy Morgan.

Three cups sugar.   One cup water.
Boil to thick, clear syrup, or until it begins to be brittle. Pour this boiling hot over the well beaten whites of three eggs: stir the mixture very briskly; pour the sugar in slowly; beat until it thickens Flavor with Chapman & Smith's lemon or vanilla.

FIG DRESSING FOR CAKE.
Mrs. R. A. Wilson.

Three-fourths lb. figs. One-half lb. raisins.
Fifteen almonds.
Cut the figs in a pan and put two or three tablespoons of boiling water over them, cover closely, and let them heat through. Have the raisins seeded, almonds blanched, add the figs and chop all fine.

ICING.
Mrs. R. A. Wilson.

One cup pulverized sugar with enough water to set to boiling. Boil to a thick syrup and add slowly the white of one egg, well beaten. Pour half the icing over the fruit to make it stick together. The other half of the icing will give the cake the first coat of icing. Cover the entire cake with icing if desired.

To be used with any white cake recipe.

CARAMEL FROSTING.
Mrs. Gilmore.

One and a half cups of brown sugar, one cup of sweet cream. Boil until very thick, having one white of an egg beat stiff, gradually beat the warm mixture in it. Chapman & Smith's vanilla flavoring. Use any white cake recipe.

CAKES.

TUTTI-FRUTTI ICING.

One pound sugar.   One gill of water.
Whites of two eggs.
Half lb. almonds, blanched and chopped.
One-fourth lb. raisins swollen in hot water.
One-fourth lb. citron, finely chopped.
Boil sugar and water until thick and waxy; pour into the whites, beat until cool; then mix the fruit and stir it in.

CARAMEL FILLING FOR WHITE CAKE.

Two cups dark brown sugar, one-half cup butter, one-half cup sweet cream, stir butter and sugar together, then add cream, boil all together until when you try it in water you can take it upon your finger like molasses; as you take it from the stove put in one teaspoon of vanilla, set in a basin of cold water and stir until you are ready to put it on the cake. This is sufficient for three layers.

BOILED ICING.

One cup granulated sugar boiled in one-half cup water until it will hair, have the white of one egg beaten to a stiff froth, keep beating with the egg beater while the syrup is slowly poured in; can be used at once.

PANSY CAKE.

This is an exceedingly pretty cake of four colors —brown, white, red and yellow. It requires two mixings:

Two-thirds cup of butter beaten to a cream, with one cup of sugar, one-half cup of milk, yolks of five eggs well beaten, one teaspoon baking powder sifted with two cups of flour. Divide and flavor one-half with half a teaspoon of orange water, for yellow cake. To the other half add half a teaspoon of vanilla and enough chocolate to color a good brown. Bake each in jelly cake pans.

The poetry of earth is never dead.

Half cup of butter, one and a half cups sugar, one-half cup sweet milk, whites of five eggs, one teaspoon baking powder sifted with two cups of flour. Divide and flavor one-half with half a teaspoon rose water for white layer, and the other half with a half teaspoon of lemon and red fruit coloring which comes in bottles and is sold by Scott Bros. When the four layers are baked, place the brown first, then the white, then red, then yellow—putting either jelly or frosting between each layer, also on the top.

This is very nice for children's parties.

NUT DRESSING.
Mrs. Wilbur S. Walker.

One cup sour cream and milk, one cup granulated sugar, one heaping cup chopped hickory nuts. Boil all together until jell-like, then remove from the stove and whip until cool.

ICE CREAM CAKE.
Mrs. O. J. Blackburn.

Two cups pulverized sugar.   One cup sweet milk.
Three-fourths cup butter.   One cup corn starch.
Two cups flour,   Whites seven eggs.
    Two teaspoons baking powder.

Put together with boiled icing, using two cups sugar and two eggs, adding one-half teaspoon tartaric acid.

POLYNAISE CAKE.
Mrs. Eliza Smith.

Make a white cake, bake in four layers.

Filling No. 1—Make an ordinary custard, divide into three parts, into the first part put half cup of currants chopped very fine; flavor with lemon.

No. 2—Stir half cup or more raisins chopped very fine, three tablespoons grated chocolate; flavor custard with vanilla.

Wise men never sit and wail their loss.

No. 3—Fill with chopped almonds, flavor with lemon and vanilla; sugar to taste.

SMALL CAKES.

CREAM PUFFS.

Into half a pint of cold water stir until smooth one and a half cups of flour, turn the same into h spider with a small cup of butter, cook and stir all the time until done; when cooled, add four beaten eggs, beat well and drop the dough in small round balls on a tin, so that they will not touch one another, and bake them; they will then probably be hollow balls; cool them on a paper soon as possible, so they will not sweat.

For filling—Take half a pint of milk, two beaten eggs, half a cup of corn starch, rub them smooth, and add a cup of sugar. Cook it in a tin pail set in a kettle of hot water, stir well; when cool, flavor with lemon. Open the puffs with a sharp knife and insert the custard.

HICKORY NUT MACAROONS.
Nellie Reichard.

One pound of sugar, One pound hickorynuts,
Three eggs, Three tablespoons flour,

Beat all well together, and drop with a spoon on a well greased pan. Bake in a slow oven.

HICKORY NUT DROP CAKES.
Anna Owens.

Two coffee cups sugar, One coffee cup butter,
Three eggs, One cup sour cream.

Two teaspoons soda stirred into the cream.
One teaspoon baking powder stirred into the flour.
Three and one-half cups of flour.
One cup of nuts. Flavor to taste·

Wit is a dangerous weapon.

HICKORY NUT KISSES.
Mrs. H. B. Smith.

Three eggs (whites,) Two cups of nuts, Cup and one-half pulverized sugar. Grease paper with butter and bake in a moderate oven.

CRULLERS.

One pint milk, Two cups sugar,
One cup butter, Three eggs,
Two teaspoons cream tartar, One teaspoon soda, A little salt. Nutmeg or cinnamon, or both, for flavoring. Fry in hot lard.

EXCELLENT GINGER SNAPS.

Boil together one pint molasses, One cup of butter, One tablespoon ginger. Let them only boil up once then set aside to cool, when cold, roll two teaspoons of soda perfectly smooth and beat into the molasses; while foaming, pour into just as little flour as will make it possible to roll out very thin. Bake quickly.

PLAIN COOKIES.
Mrs. Geo. Babcock.

Two cups sugar, One cup butter,
One cup rich sour cream, Two eggs,
One teaspoon soda. Mix soft.

FRUIT COOKIES.
Mrs. Geo. Babcock.

Two cups brown sugar, One cup of butter, One and one-half cups seeded raisins, Three tablespoons sour milk, One teaspoon soda, One tablespoon cinnamon, One nutmeg, Two eggs, three and one-half cups of flour, or enough to make quite stiff. Drop on pan to bake.

He is well paid that is well satisfied.

CAKES.

GINGER COOKIES.
Mrs. Geo. Babcock.

One cup butter, One cup light brown sugar,
One cup N.O. molasses, One cup sour cream,
One tablespoon ginger, Two teaspoons soda.
Mix soft.

GINGER SNAPS WITHOUT EGGS.
Mrs. Mira L. Miller.

Two cups molases, One cup sugar,
One cup sour milk, One cup butter,
One heaping teaspoon soda,
One teaspoon ginger,
One teaspoon ground cinnamon,
Flour to roll. Don't knead much. Bake in quick oven.

FRUIT COOKIES.
Mrs E. P. Clarke.

One and one-half cups sugar,
One-third cup lard, or butter and lard mixed,
One-half cup sweet milk, Two eggs,
Two teaspoons baking powder,
One cup stoned raisins,
One teaspoon each of all kinds spices,
Add flour until stiff enough to roll.

GINGER COOKIES.
Mrs. Duke.

One cup molasses, One cup sugar,
One cup sweet milk, Nine tablespoons lard,
One teaspoon each of salt, cinnamon, alum and soda. Mix as soft as possible to roll out.

GINGER PUFFS.
Mrs. Henry Ewing.

One cup N. O. molasses, One cup sugar,
One cup water, One-half cup butter,
Four and one-half cups flour,
One tablespoon ginger, One tablespoon soda.

Question your desires.

CAKES.

GINGERBREAD.
Alta M. Claycomb.

One cup molasses,   One cup sugar,
One-half cup butter,   One cup milk,
Three eggs,   Two teaspoons soda,
Two teaspoons ginger, Two teaspoons spices,
    Four cups flour.

GINGERBREAD.
Alice Duer.

One cup sugar,   One cup N. O. molasses,
One cup sour cream,   One cup butter,
Four cups flour,   Three eggs, well beaten,
One tablespoon ginger, One tablespoon soda,
    One lemon, grated rind and juice.

GOSSAMER GINGERBREAD.
Mrs. Harry B. Smith.

One cup butter,   Two cups sugar,
    (well beaten)
One cup milk,   One tablespoon ginger,
    Three and two-thirds cups flour,

Drop one tablespoon on tin and spread with knife as thin as possible. Bake in well but not over heated oven.

P. S. Use pans upside down, cut and remove before it cools. Cut about four inches long by one and one-half wide.

SOFT GINGERBREAD.
Mrs. Mary Patterson.

One cup molasses,   One cup sugar,
One cup butter,   One cup sweet milk,
Four cups flour,   Four eggs,
    One tablespoon ginger,
One small teaspoon soda dissolved in the milk;

Beat the molasses, butter, sugar and spices to a cream, whip in the beaten yolks with the milk and

---

Every man is odd.

lastly the whites, alternating with the flour, bake in two loaves.

LOAF GINGERBREAD.

One cup butter, Two cups molasses,
One tablespoon ginger, Two eggs well beaten,
One heaping teaspoon soda,
One cup sour cream.
Flour to make as thick as pound cake.

GINGER CAKE.
Theo Sexton.

One cup molasses, One teaspoon ginger,
One-half cup water, One teaspoon soda,
One-half cup butter, One egg,
Two and one-half cups flour,
One cup raisins,
Salt, and flavor with Chapman & Smith's delicious spice extracts.

Beat soda in molasses, then butter, the beaten egg, one cup flour, water, then second cup flour.

RAISED DOUGHNUTS.
Mrs. L. Marks.

Two cups bread sponge, Butter size of egg,
Three-fourths cups sugar, One egg,

Mix soft as can be handled. Let raise once then cut and when very light fry in hot lard.

DOUGHNUTS.
Mrs. Mary Pillsbury.

Two cups sugar, Two eggs,
One tablespoon butter, Two cups sour milk,
One teaspoon soda, Flour to mix well.
Use nutmeg to flavor.

RAISED DOUGHNUTS.
Mrs. D. D. Diffenbaugh.

Take light dough the size of a small loaf bread, work into this one cup butter and lard mixed.

Who speaks not truly, lies.

Two eggs beaten in one pint sugar. Mix thoroughly in the dough and knead but not as stiff as bread. Let rise then work down, lay on the board and cut out and let the dough get very light and fry in hot lard adding cinnamon to flavor.

DOUGHNUTS.
Mrs. A. P. Graham.

One cup sour cream,   One cup sugar,
                 One teaspoon soda,

Three eggs beaten separately and flour enough to roll nicely. Use just as you want them. Dough will keep for weeks. Last is better than first.

COOKIES.
Mrs. Ida Weir.

Three eggs,   Three cups sugar,
    Half cup sour milk with soda,
One cup butter,   Half cup lard,

Make thin dough and bake in hot oven.

BREAKFAST GINGER COOKIES.
Mrs. W. T. Wiley.

Two cups N. O. molasses,   One cup of sugar,
One cup sour milk,   One cup of lard,
Four teaspoons soda—one put in the milk the rest in the flour—One tablespoon ginger, two eggs, pinch of salt. Roll out thick.

JELLY BISCUIT.

Take Boston crackers (they are the best) and drop them for a second in boiling hot water—it is better to put them in and take them instantly out—then dip them at once into beaten egg and fry in boiling lard. They should only be a delicate brown. When finished they will be the shape of egg biscuit, the outside edge curling up and forming a little saucer. Into this saucer drop a tea-

Unstained thoughts do seldom dream of evil.

spoon of jelly or preserve. Preserved figs are very nice for the purpose. This makes a very dainty, delicate and quickly prepared dish for lunch or dessert. Squares of bread, lightly browned in the same way, are delicious. If using bread, substitute cold milk for hot water.

TEA CAKES.

One small cup sugar, One large tablespoon butter, Half cup sweet milk, One egg beaten separately' Flour enough to make batter—about one cup, One teaspoon Chapman & Smith's Chicago Yeast powder, flavor with lemon. Bake in gem pans.

RAISIN PUFFS.
Mrs. L. M. Dougherty.

Five tablespoons sugar, Half cup of butter,
One cup sweet milk, Two eggs,
Two teaspoons baking powder,
One cup raisins seeded,
Flour to make as stiff as cake dough; put in cups and steam one-half hour. Serve with lemon sauce.

FRIED CAKES.
Mrs. Addie Morton.

One quart flour, Three eggs,
One cup sugar, One cup milk,
Six teaspoons baking powder,
Six teaspoons hot lard,
A little flour and salt.
When all mixed, set in oven and heat through before adding hot lard. Mix soft.

Ignorance is the curse of God.

Henry Patterson
COLD STORAGE.
111 and 113 East First Avenue.

Jobbers of Butter, Eggs, Poultry, Green Fruits and Vegetables.

☞ Try a few bottles of the

Celebrated Colfax Mineral Water.

OUR RECEIPTS.

For $5 we will be glad to give any one a *Receipt* for one year's subscription to THE DAILY REVIEW; or for half that amount a *Receipt* for a six months' subscription. Or, if preferred, *Receipts* will be given for any shorter time on *Receipt* of Ten Cents for each week for which the paper is wanted. If you are not situated so you can get The Daily Review promptly, for $1.50 we will give you a *Receipt* for one year's subscription to THE SEMI-WEEKLY REVIEW.

YOUR RECEIPTS If you take advantage of any of our *Receipts* you will be in *Receipt* of all the news of importance occuring in Monmouth and Warren County, or in the world for that matter, though the home news is given the preference.

Try It and See.   **REVIEW PRINTING CO.**

Root

The Photographer
The Largest Gallery in the City.

Ground Flour.   213 South Main St.

THE MODEL.

A glance at our stock will tell you at once where to trade.

Fine Clothing a specialty,
And headquarters for **Gent's Furnishing Goods.**

PEN D. GOOD, MAN'G'R.   **MODEL CLOTHING CO.**

BEVERAGES.

"Anon, we'll drink a measure
The table round."—*Macbeth*.

GOOD COFFEE.

There are four essentials to good coffee—the best coffee, an egg, cream and a clean coffee pot. The coffee pot should be emptied, washed and scalded and dried every time it is used

Take one tablespoon of best coffee for each person and half a pint of water, let it boil five minutes, then remove from the fire at once.

To make coffee for twenty persons use one and one-half pints of ground coffee. Mix with egg and cold water and put in cheesecloth bag. Pour over one gallon boiling water. Let stand where it keeps hot. Serve with whipped cream.

TEA.

Scald tea pot and put tea in while hot, using one teaspoon of tea for each person (if strong tea is desired,) to one-half pint boiling water Let stand a few moments before serving.

ICED TEA.

Make strong tea. After standing a few moments to extract strength, pour off and let cool. Add water to desired strength. Pour over cracked ice and serve with sliced lemon.

C. Shultz. Extract of Beef. All kinds of foods for invalids.

RUSSIAN TEA.

Pare and slice good juicy lemons and lay a piece in the bottom of each cup; sprinkle with white sugar, and pour hot, strong tea upon it. Do not use cream.

CHOCOLATE.

Dissolve three tablespoons of scraped chocolate, or equal parts of chocolate and cocoa, in a pint of boiling water and boil for fifteen minutes; add one pint of rich milk; let scald and serve hot.

CHOCOLATE—VIENNA STYLE.

Four ounces of chocolate, one quart milk, three tablespoons of hot water, and one tablespoon of sugar.

Cut the chocolate in fine bits. Put the milk on the stove in the double boiler, and when heated to the boiling point, put the chocolate, sugar and water in a small iron or granite-ware pan, and stir over a hot fire until smooth and glossy. Stir this mixture into the hot milk, and beat well with a whisk. Serve at once, putting a tablespoon of whipped cream in each cup and then filling up with the chocolate.

The plain chocolate may be used instead of the vanilla, but in that case use a teaspoon of vanilla extract and three generous tablespoons of sugar instead of one.

BLACKBERRY CORDIAL.

Secure ripe berries and crush them; to each gallon of juice add one quart of boiling water; let it stand twenty-four hours, stirring it a few times; strain and add two pounds of sugar to each gallon of liquid; put in jugs and cork tightly. It may be used in two months, is excellent for summer complaint, and can be taken by delicate invalids.

A light heart lives long.

STRAWBERRY SHERBET

Crush a pound of strawberries into a basin and add a quart of water, with a sliced lemon, let it stand for two or three hours. Put one and a quarter pounds of sugar into another basin ; cover the basin with a cloth and through this cloth strain the strawberry juice ; when the sugar is fully dissolved, strain again, and set the vessel into which it is strained on ice until ready to serve.

TOAST WATER.

Brown nicely but do not burn the slices of bread, and pour upon them sufficient boiling water to cover Let them steep until cold, keeping the bowl or dish containing the toast closely covered. Strain off the water and sweeten to taste. Cool with ice

FLAXSEED LEMONADE.

Pour on four tablespoons of whole flaxseed, one quart of boiling water and add the juice of two lemons. Let it steep for three hours, keeping it closely covered. Sweeten to taste. Excellent for colds.

SLIPPERY-ELM BARK TEA.

Pour boiling water over the bark, first breaking it into bits ; cover the pitcher containing it and let it stand until cold ; add lemon juice if desired and sweeten to taste.

MULLED BUTTERMILK.

The well-beaten yolk of an egg added to boiling buttermilk and allowed to boil up ; or add to the boiling buttermilk a little thickening of flour and cold buttermilk.

There's a small choice in rotten apples.

BEVERAGES.

BEEF TEA.

Mince one pound of good lean beef and put into a jar with one teacup of cold water; cork closely and set in a boiler or steamer to cook. It will require three or four hours. Strain and season.

BOUILLON,

To one pound of round steak add one and one-half tumblers of cold water, cut the beef in small pieces, cover and let simmer until the substance is all out the meat, then strain and return to the stove to keep hot. Beat two eggs in a bowl, turn the broth on gradually, stirring all the time. Salt to taste. This is good for dyspeptics.

CORN MEAL GRUEL.

Two tablespoons corn meal wet in cold water; add to three pints boiling water, a little salt and boil twenty-five minutes,

CELERY TEA.

Use celery freely. A tea made of the leaves and roots and used freely is said to cure rheumatism.

BEATEN EGG FOR THE SICK.

Take one fresh egg, one tablespoon of ice cold water, one teaspoon sugar; beat very light. then add two tablespoons of cream.

OAT MEAL GRUEL.

Add to one cup well cooked oat meal while hot, one cup of milk and one cup of hot water; beat all thoroughly together and strain through a wire strainer; if desired a little salt can be added.

Boiled milk with a little salt added to make it palatable, is one of the most healthful drinks. It sooths an irritated stomach, nourishes the flesh tissues and tends to make the complexion clear.

Keep thy pen from lender's books.

REFRESHING DRINK FOR THE SICK.

One-third of a glass of raspberry juice, mix with two-thirds of a glass of ice water. Sweeten to suit the taste of the person.

Blackberry, currant or strawberry juice may be used the same way. All are delicious.

FOR DRYNESS OF MOUTH OR THROAT.

Take a tablespoon of pulverized slippery-elm and pour half a pint of boiling water on it, sweeten and ice it. Take a teaspoonfull as often as twenty minutes.

H. Burlingim

Keeps Chapman & Smith's Extracts, Yeast Powder and Cleaned Currants.

We are born to do benefits.

MONMOUTH COLLEGE,

MONMOUTH, ILLINOIS.

Opens First Wednesday in September.

Five courses of study, including Music. Intruction in all departments by thoroughly competent teachers.

Send for catalogue and other information to

J. B. McMICHAEL,
PRESIDENT.

Breakfast Dishes.

"And then to breakfast with what appetite you have."
—*Henry VIII.*

MOCK SAUSAGE.

Soak dry bread in water. Chop equal amount of any kind of cold meat fine. Season with salt, pepper and sage. Make in little cakes and fry.

MUFFINS.
Miss Fannie Adams, Burlington, Ia.

One quart of flour, four teaspoons baking powder, four eggs beaten separately very light, milk to make a batter thicker than griddle cake; salt, one tablespoon of melted butter put into the milk.

RAISED WAFFLES.
Mrs. B.

One pint of new milk with flour to make a thin batter, add one cup of yeast, two well beaten eggs and half a cup of butter or the size of an egg, beat this very light and add flour to make a stiff batter, and let raise over night.

BUNS.

One-half cup melted butter, one cup sugar, one cup sugar, one cup yeast, one cup warm water or new milk, half cup "Rolling Pin" cleaned currants. Beat light and add flour to make as stiff as biscuit dough and let this rise all night. Mould and put in pans to rise for twenty minutes and bake for breakfast. Add a little salt when mixing.

Love all, trust a few.

CROQUETTES OF COLD STEAK
Mrs. F. P. Gilbert.

Take bits of cold steak and mince very fine. Add three or four chopped cold potatoes. Season with pepper add salt. Mix this thoroughly and then add a beaten egg. Press into cakes, roll in cracker crumbs and fry in hot lard.

PARSNIP FRITTERS.

Boil five or six medium size parsnips till tender, mash very fine, add one-half cup of milk, a tablespoon of butter, two eggs, a tablespoon of flour, a little salt; fry a delicate brown in hot drippings; serve on a hot dish.

APPLE FRITTERS.

To the recipe for fritters add one cup chopped apples.

Oyster Fritters—add oysters.

MUFFINS.
Sadie Neville.

Two tablespoons of butter, two tablespoons sugar. Cream the butter and sugar until very smooth, two cups flour, adding one and one-half teaspoon baking powder, sift thoroughly, two eggs, one cup sweet milk, salt; after creaming the butter and sugar in the bowl, mix very quick and bake from fifteen to twenty minutes in gem pans in a pretty hot oven.

PUFF OVERS.
Mrs. Wildemuth.

Yolks of two eggs well beaten, three-fourths cup sweet milk, one teaspoon melted butter, one-half teaspoon salt, one teaspoon sugar, one and one-half cups flour, two teaspoons Chicago yeast powder, whites of two eggs. Bake in gem tins.

Speak less than thou knowest,

A SIMPLE AND DELICIOUS MUFFIN.
Mrs. J. W. Matthews.

Take a piece of butter the size of an egg, mix with it one tablespoon white sugar, add one egg, three-fourths teacup sweet milk, one large pint flour with which has been sifted one teaspoon Chicago yeast powder. Put into a well buttered pie pan; bake one-half hour in a moderate oven. Eaten hot with butter it is very nice for breakfast or lunch. It may be made of graham flour wholly or in part. Buttered muffin rings can be used if preferred.

SNOW FLAKE TOAST.
Mrs. Jas. French.

Heat to boiling one quart milk to which one-half cup of cream and a little salt have been added. Thicken with a tablespoon of flour rubbed smooth in a little cold milk. Have ready the whites of two eggs beaten to a stiff froth and when the sauce is cooked turn a cup of it on the beaten eggs stirring constantly so it will form a light, frothy mixture, to which add the rest of the sauce; keep hot but do not allow to boil. Serve on slices of zwieback or toast previously moistened with milk or hot water.

RICE CRUMPET.

One coffee cup boiled rice, two coffee cups flour, one cup milk, two eggs, two tablespoons sugar, scant, one tablespoon melted butter, pinch of salt, one teaspoon Chicago yeast powder. Let rise over night, in the morning lift carefully into gem pans, let stand fifteen minutes and bake quickly.

A TASTY BREAKFAST DISH.

Take a few slices of Morrell's "Iowa's Pride" breakfast bacon (be sure and cut them very thin.)

"Have more than thou showest."—King Lear.

Cut off the skin before putting it in the frying pan. Have frying pan quite hot before the bacon is put in. Keep the bacon turned to prevent curling up, until both sides show a light brown. Take out at once and serve hot.

RICE BATTER CAKES.
Mrs. Mary A. Frantz.

Three tea cups butter, four eggs, salt, one tumbler cooked rice. Beat eggs thoroughly, make all into a batter the usual thickness for batter cakes; add one teaspoon soda dissolved in warm water.

HASH CAKE.

Chop fine such bits of cold meat as you may have, add a double quantity of potato chopped fine also; mix well, season with pepper and salt to taste; eight minutes before you wish to serve the dish, melt a tablespoonful of butter in a spider and when hissing hot, put in the hash and press it down well and evenly all around. At the end of the time specified, have a heated plate ready, turn it over the spider, tip the latter upside down with the plate beneath, send your steaming hash cake to the table.

WAFFLES.
Margaret Owens.

Mix well three cups flour with one-half cup butter, one teaspoon salt, two teaspoons Chicago yeast powder, one quart milk, yolks three eggs. Stir well; add last the whites of the eggs well beaten.

WAFFLES.
Mrs. H. M. Graham.

One pint sweet milk, three eggs well beaten, one teaspoon baking powder, one tablespoon melted butter, salt; stir in flour enough to make batter; add the melted butter the last thing. Bake on hot, well greased waffle irons. Serve with hot maple syrup.

Lend less than thou owest."—King Lear.

CORN MEAL MUFFINS.
Sadie Neville.

Two tablespoons butter, two tablespoons sugar, one cup pastry flour, one cup good corn meal (fine ground), two teaspoons Chicago yeast powder, one generous cup milk, two eggs. Cream the butter and sugar, add the other ingredients and stir rapidly; the eggs must be well beaten. Add salt to the eggs before beating.

CORN BREAD.
Emma Gregg, Chicago.

Two cups corn meal, sifted; one cup flour, two eggs, two cups sweet milk, four teaspoons melted butter, one tablespoon sugar, two teaspoon yeast powder; add a little salt.

BREAKFAST DISH.

Heat a can of salmon, season with pepper and salt, and place on thin slices of buttered toast, heat a large coffee cup of milk or cream, salt and thicken a little with flour; if milk is used add a piece of butter and pour over fish and toast.

THANKSGIVING HASH.

Take a dish suitable for the table, place a layer of bread crumbs in the bottom, then a layer of chopped turkey, next a layer of oysters, so on until the dish is filled, pour over one pint of cream sauce, bake quickly for twenty minutes.

CODFISH BALLS.

Boil potatoes and mash. pick up codfish very fine and pour over it boiling water, let stand until soft, then add potatoes, having one-half as much fish as potato. one egg well beaten, two tablespoons cream, a little pepper, salt and butter; fry before the mixture gets cold.

"Sweets grown common lose their dear delights."
—*102d Sonnet.*

CREAM TOAST.

Brown bread nicely on both sides, let one pint sweet cream come to a boil, add one tablespoon of butter, a little salt, pour over toast and serve at once.

BREAKFAST DISH.

Slice three or four ripe bananas in a dish and squeeze over them the juice of a good-sized lemon, then put over this a gill of ice water and a half cup of granulated sugar, stand where it will get good and cold, and after half an hour it will be ready to serve. The lemons take away the naturally insipid taste, and are healthy.

EGGS.

"Things well done
And with a care, exempt themselves from fear."
—*Henry VIII.*

EGGS.

Three minutes will boil them soft.

Five minutes will cook whites hard, but not yolks.

Eight minutes will cook both.

To boil an egg to perfection use Camm's egg cups.

PICKLED EGGS.

Boil three or four dozen hard, remove shells. To one quart of vinegar put allspice, ginger and two cloves of garlic; boil, when spiced to taste pour over eggs. Nice for picnics.

Welcome ever smiles, and farewell goes out sighing.

Premier Egg Cups

E. I. CAMM.

JEWELER

The Egg is in it.
Made of China.
Durable. Pretty.
1 and 2 Egg Sizes.
No Shells.
No Uncertainty.
Pat. June 13, '93.

Every well regulated family should secure some of these little

Egg Cups

if they wish to relish a good wholesome breakfast. Considered by all epicures as the only way to cook eggs. Sold by

BREAK THE EGG into the cup, screw on the cover and boil the egg in this China cup instead of the shell, and serve the egg in the same China cup.

E. I. CAMM,
Who always keeps a full line of everything found in a first-class Jewelry establishment.

MOTHERS!

When the boys need anything in the way of

CLOTHING

You will do well to see our stock, as we always carry a large line in Suits and Overcoats: also, the MOTHERS' FRIEND WAIST in all grades. Ask to see the

Boys' Iron-Clad Black Cotton Hose.

In HATS and CAPS we always have the newest and the nobbiest styles in the market.

☞ ALWAYS THE BEST AT ☜

One Price to All.   **PHILIP NUSBAUM'S.**

STUFFED EGGS.

Eight eggs, four teaspoons potted ham, one-half teaspoon lemon juice, one teaspoon creamed butter, add a little cayenne pepper, salt to taste; rub yolks of eggs through a sieve.

BAKED EGGS.

Butter your gem pans, dredge with cracker crumbs, break an egg in each cup, put a small piece of butter on top of each egg, dust over with cracker crumbs, and bake in oven; turn them out on hot platter.

DEVILED EGGS.

Boil eggs hard, cut in two and slip out the yolks. Mash yolks fine, season to taste with pepper, salt, butter, vinegar and mustard and press back into the white. Nice for picnics.

EGG SANDWICHES.

Cut thin slices of bread, and butter evenly. Boil six eggs hard and remove the yolks; mash until soft and add one teaspoon melted butter, a little vinegar, and pinch of salt: chop whites fine and mix and spread on bread. Cut in fancy shapes; serve on platter with parsley.

BAKED EGGS.
Mrs. W. Q. Bell.

Delicious—Twelve eggs, boil hard, cut in two, take the yolks and mash fine, add a large spoonful butter, one cup powdered crackers, one and one-half cups milk, season with pepper and salt; put the whites in a baking dish, pour this mixture over and bake fifteen minutes.

POACHED EGGS.
Mrs. W. Q. Bell.

Serve poached eggs in slices of fried bread that are previously covered with the finest mince of hot

What's more miserable than discontent."—Henry VI.

(warmed over) meat. This is a substantial yet dainty dish for luncheon. Make the meat a mince of chicken or turkey, and add a few chopped truffles around the well-formed eggs, and you have a dainty French dish.

EGGS SUR LE PLAT.

Beat two eggs separately. spread upon the platter, then drop as many eggs upon this as are required at the meal, season with salt and pepper, sprinkle over with cracker crumbs, and place in a hot oven for a few moments when it is ready for the table.

OMELET FOR BREAKFAST.

Beat four eggs separately, into the yolks put one cup of milk, one tablespoon of flour, salt and pepper lastly, add the whites of eggs, bake in a deep dish about ten minutes in a hot oven.

PICKLES AND CATSUPS.

"I warrant there's vinegar and pepper in it"
—*Twelfth Night.*

PICKLED APPLES.
Mrs. J. Shultz.

Take ripe, hard, sweet apples, peel evenly, cut in halves and core. To a peck of apples take about two quarts of vinegar and four pounds of sugar, half an ounce of mace, half an ounce of cloves and the same of allspice, all unground, a few grains of pepper and a little salt. Heat the vinegar and sugar together till it boils, skim well, put the spices in a thin muslin bag and add to the vinegar, then put in the apples. Place over the

---

C. Shultz, Pure Spices.

A word we wish with every cook
Who looks within this precious book ;
Each RECIPE will please, we're sure,
If every dish is clean and pure.
Before you mix we truly hope
You'll freely use "SELF-WASHING SOAP;"
The largest bar of soap in town
We think is "MAPLE CITY BROWN;"
"SUPERIOR GERMAN" must eclipse,
The same is true of "LAUNDRY CHIPS;"
The "ALPHA" comes a little late
But takes its place by big "DOWN WEIGHT."
We make these soaps much work to save,
And "BARBERS' BAR" for men who shave.
Now if you would be neat and clean
And always ready to be seen,
"MONMOUTH OAT MEAL" we recommend,
"MAPLE BOQUET" will prove a friend,
With "COCHIN COCOA" or "PINE TAR,"
Or with "ROSE BUD" a lovely bar,
Or with our "AMBER GLYCERINE,"
The clearest we have ever seen;
Or with our "MAPLE CITY TAR,"
Or with our nice big "FIVE CENT BAR,"
You'll get results that always please,
And meet your guests with perfect ease,
Why use a soap of doubtful worth,
When we've the best that's made on earth,
For MAPLE CITY SOAPS are pure
And they will please you we are sure.

fire and stew slowly till the apples are soft. Then take out the apples, let the vinegar boil down and pour it over the fruit; cover and put away.

CUCUMBER PICKLES.
Mrs. H. W. Sisson.

First—Take small, fresh cucumbers, put into strong brine and let stand twenty-four hours. After draining well, fill quart jars (pack closely.)

Second—With good cider vinegar add sugar and cinnamon bark to taste, and one small red pepper for each quart, heat, bringing almost to a boil, not boiling, and pour over pickles each day for three days, sealing closely each time.

CUCUMBER PICKLES.
Mrs. Nettie Hess.

Two hundred cucumbers, cover with water, add a pint of salt. In the morning drain off the water, take as much vinegar as you had of water, one ounce each of whole cloves and allspice, and a piece of alum the size of a walnut. Heat all together, and pour boiling hot over the cucumbers. Adding sugar to the vinegar makes nice sweet pickles.

CHERRY BUTTER.
Mrs. Mary Pillsbury.

Wash the cherries and stem them. Boil until soft, then rub through a colander. To each pint of pulp add a pint of sugar, boil until thick like other fruit butters. Can them or keep in closely covered jars.

RASPBERRY JAM.

Raspberry jam is much better if one-third or one-half cherries are used.

CRANBERRY JELLY.

Pare, quarter and core twelve large tart apples, (greenings, or any juicy apples preferred), put in

Friendships' full of dregs.

a porcelain kettle with two quarts cranberries, stew till soft, then strain through jelly bag, heat juice, add two pounds of sugar. and boil until it jellies. Has much better flavor than when made simply of cranberries.

COLD CATSUP.

One peck of ripe tomatoes, sliced fine, sprinkle with salt and let stand two hours. When drained add two grated horseradishes, one small teaspoon of salt. one teacup of granulated sugar, two tablespoons black pepper. two tablespoons cinnamon, one teacup chopped onions, six bunches celery cut fine. two red peppers without seeds. four pints vinegar. Make cold and can.

CHOPPED PICKLES.
Margaret Holt.

One peck of green tomatoes. half peck of onions, one head of cabbage, one pound of white mustard seed, one ounce each of tumeric, celery seed and cinnamon, half ounce of cloves, one pound of sugar, one pint of grated horseradish, six large green peppers. Slice the tomatoes. let stand over night. sprinkle a handful of salt over them. press all the water out. chop all fine. Mix all ingredients and cook in vinegar enough to cover them. until the tomatoes look clear.

PEACH PICKLES.
Mabel Pillsbury.

One quart best cider vinegar, three pints sugar boil slowly five minutes and skim. Pare fruit (free-stones), put in the syrup together with spices in the proportion of two teaspoons whole cloves, four tablespoons cinnamon, and a small piece of ginger root to each gallon of fruit. Simmer until the peaches can be pierced through with silver fork. Fill fruit jars with the fruit and set in warm

"Angels are bright still, though the brightest fell."

place. Boil the syrup until like thin molasses; skim out spices, and fill the jars with the boiling syrup. Seal immediately.

TOMATO CATSUP.
Mrs. Edgar MacDill.

One-half bushel of nice, ripe tomatoes, cut in small pieces, put in a large kettle, add two large onions, let boil until tender; rub through sieve, place back in the kettle, adding one quart of good cider vinegar, one-half pint of salt; sweeten to taste; five cents' worth of whole cloves, cinnamon, allspice, mustard seed, black pepper; put spices in a thin bag, tie up, boil them with tomatoes, boil two hours, or until a little thick, stirring constantly; seal tight in bottles.

OIL PICKLES.
Mrs. Eunice Marks.

Cut cucumbers in thin slices without paring, one-fourth peck onions to two gallons cucumbers. After all are sliced let lie in salt water over night, then drain in separate colanders. Three tablespoons ground black pepper, quarter lb. ground mustard, one red pepper cut in bits, half pint good salad oil. Mix oil, mustard and pepper, and pour into as much cider vinegar as will cover pickles. Cover closely to exclude air and keep in cool place. (Good thanksgiving.) One dozen cucumbers make a gallon after they are sliced.

TOMATO CATSUP.
Adeline P. Holt.

Half bushel of ripe tomatoes, peel and slice tomatoes and stew in their own liquor until soft, then rub through a seive fine enough to retain the seeds, put over the fire and when it is boiling add four ounces salt, three ounces ground black pepper, one ounce of cinnamon, one half ounce ground cloves, and drachm cayenne pepper, one teacup

Keep on hand "Rolling Pin" Cleaned Currants.

sugar, one quart good cider vinegar, boil down until thick, stirring all the time to prevent burning. Bottle while hot.

MEAT SAUCE.
Mary Mason.

Half bushel green tomatoes, half peck onions, one dozen green peppers, two gallons vinegar, two lbs. brown sugar, spice to suit taste. Cook on slow fire two hours.

CUCUMBER CATSUP.
Mrs. Wm. Mitchell.

Three dozen cucumbers, one and a half dozen onions chopped fine, three fourths cup salt sprinkled over them and put in colander with a weight on top and drain over night, add one tea cup white mustard seed, one-half tea cup ground black pepper; mix well and put in bottles two-thirds full and fill to the top with good cold cider vinegar; seal like any other catsup.

SPICED GRAPES.

Five pounds of grapes, three pounds granulated sugar, one-half pint vinegar, two teaspoons each of cinnamon and allspice, half teaspoon cloves; pulp the grapes, boil the skins until tender, cook the pulp soft, and strain through a sieve, add it to the skins, put in the spices, sugar, and vinegar, boil thoroughly and then seal.

MUSTARD PICKLE.
Mrs. James French.

One quart each of small whole cucumbers, large cucumbers sliced, green tomatoes sliced and small button onions; one large cauliflower divided into flowrets, and four green peppers cut fine. Make a brine of four quarts of water and one pint of salt. Pour it over the mixture of vegetables. Let

Use Maple City Soaps.

them stand for twenty-four hours. Heat just enough to scald it, and turn into a colander to drain. Mix one cup flour; six tablespoons ground mustard and one tablespoon of tumeric with enough cold vinegar to make a smooth paste; then add a cup of sugar, and sufficient vinegar to make two quarts in all. Boil this mixture until it thickens and is smooth, stirring all the time. Add the vegetables, and cook until well heated through. Put into jars or bottles and seal.

SPICED CHERRIES.

Five quarts seeded cherries without the juice, mix five pounds sugar over night, pour off the juice for three mornings, boil and skim, each time pouring on the cherries boiling hot, the fourth time add whole spices to taste, one pint cider vinegar, boil down with enough juice to cover cherries, add cherries, and let come to a boil.

SPICED GOOSEBERRIES.

Five pounds of the fruit, three pounds of sugar, two teaspoons cinnamon, half teaspoon allspice, half teaspoon cloves, vinegar to suit the taste; boil thoroughly and stir often to keep it from scorching.

WATER MELON SWEET PICKELS.
Linnie Brewer.

Pare the rinds, cut in pieces diamond or square shaped, take one large teaspoon of pulverized alum to as many as you can cover with water in a gallon crock—the water should taste well of the alum—let stand from twenty-four to thirty-six hours, as may be convenient, pour off the alum water, let stand in cold water thirty minutes. Should any of the pieces be soft trim it off, as they should be firm. Cover with water—may be warm but not boiling— put one cup sugar and several pieces of ginger root. let simmer but not boil hard until the pieces are clear. Try with a straw, as they become clear and tender, take out in a colander, let drain, do not wait until all are done, and don't put all in the colander at once for if crowded they will mash, thak in a large pan. When all are done weigh and soke as much sugar as fruit, make a syrup and pour over the fruit, do the same for four days, cooking the syrup each day until quite thick; on the fourth day add one quart of vinegar, two tablespoons of stick cinnamon broken in small pieces, heap the spoon and put in the syrup, one tablespoon cloves pounded and tied in a cloth, drop in and cook until it tastes well—if you like more spice you can put it in—put in the fruit and let heat through. Put up in glass jars.

WATER MELON RINDS.

Pare and cut in any shape, pour over them weak alum water, hot; let stand twenty-four hours, then pour off, rinse well, and boil in clear water until tender, make a syrup of equal measures of vinegar and sugar, some stick cinnamon and race ginger, boil the rinds in this till clear, put in jar, cover and put away.

SPANISH PICKLES.
Mrs. A. B. Seaman.

One dozen green cucumbers peeled and sliced fine, one peck green tomatoes, four heads cabbage small and solid, one dozen onions, three pints cider vinegar, three ounces white mustard seed, one ounce celery, one ounce tumeric, one-fourth pound box Coleman's mustard, one and one-half pounds of sugar. Slice all the vegetables with a cabbage slicer. Put each separately in a weak brine for an hour or two, drain in a cheese cloth, put in layers in a kettle. Mix mustard with cold vinegar adding tumeric, then gradually add boiling vinegar and sugar. Put one-third vegetables in kettle, pour on vinegar, then add another third, etc, If too moist do not use all the vinegar. Boil slowly until tender, and put in glass jars hot.

CONFECTIONERY.

"Sweets with sweets war not."—*Shakespeare's Poems*

FONDANT FOR FRENCH CANDY.
Theo Sexton.

One-half cup of water to two of granulated sugar; add a pinch of cream of tartar. Boil without stirring for ten minutes, then try by dropping a little in cold water. When it can be rolled by the fingers into a soft (not a sticky) ball, put in a cool place. When a little scum has formed over the top, beat with a wooden spoon until it becomes a soft, creamy mass. Then flavor and mould. This may be used as a foundation for any French candy. Nuts, dates and figs may be used with the fondant, making a variety. For chocolate creams, roll the fondant into small balls; let them get perfectly hard, dip them into melted chocolate to which has been added some of the hot melted fondant.

BUTTER SCOTCH.
Theo Sexton.

One cup N. O. molasses, one cup sugar, (brown or granulated) half cup butter, added when nearly done. Boil until it snaps when put in cold water. Pour into buttered tins and when cool enough mark into squares.

A good nose is requisite, to smell out work for the other senses.

BUTTER SCOTCH No. 2.

To the above recipe add one tablespoon vinegar and pinch of soda.

CREAM CANDY
Eva Clark.

Two cups of white sugar, one-half cup of water, four tablespoons of vinegar, teaspoon of butter. Boil twenty minutes; when removed from the stove add one-fourth of a teaspoon of vanilla; do not stir it. Pull.

FUDGES.
Margaret Dunbar.

To four cups granulated sugar add one-half cake Bakers' chocolate, one cup rich milk and one-fourth pound butter. Place over hot fire, stirring constantly until it becomes thick, (but not hard when put in water.) Remove from fire and stir until mass begins to set. Pour in pan making about half inch thick, and while still warm cut in squares. (Vanilla may be added.)

CHOCOLATE CARAMELS.
Mrs. H. B. Smith.

Four cups granulated sugar, one cup cold water, three tablespoons glucose. Boil until brittle, then add half cake chocolate (melted), one cup cream. Boil again until brittle. Flavor. Mark when partly cool.

NUT TAFFY.

One cup sugar, one cup vinegar with one teaspoon soda dissolved in it, one cup molasses, and a piece of butter the size of an egg. Boil till very brittle, drop in water when done; add one cup nut meats.

Best and Purest Candies at the Candy Kitchen, Southwest corner of the Square.

CONFECTIONERY.

MARSH MALLOWS.

Dissolve one-half pound of gum arabic in one pint of water, strain and add one-half pound fine sugar and place over the fire, stirring constantly until the syrup is dissolved and of the consistency of honey; add gradually the whites of four eggs, well beaten, stir the mixture until it becomes somewhat thin and does not adhere to the finger; flavor to taste, and pour into a tin slightly dusted with powdered starch. When cool divide into small squares.

SALTED ALMONDS.
Margaret Dunbar.

Blanch the almonds by throwing in hot water, then in cold, and stir through them enough butter to make them seem oily; warm them while stirring in the butter, then spread them over a baking pan and bake fifteen minutes, or till crisp, stirring often; when done sprinkle with salt while hot.

SALTED ALMONDS No. 2.

White of an egg, salt, stir in blanched almonds and brown in oven.

SALTED PEANUTS.

Peanuts may take the place of almonds; procure the raw peanuts, shell and set them on the stove in cold water and let them come to a boil and stand ten minutes, drain off and put on cold water, blanch and treat same as almonds.

"*To persist in doing wrong, extenuates not wrong.*"
—*Troilus and Cressida.*

ADDENDA.

"Jove and my stars be praised. Here is yet a postscript."
—*Twelfth Night.*

CREAM SOUP.
Mrs. Eliza B. Smith.

Boil chicken until tender; if too fat, skim; salt and pepper to taste, make thickening as for gravy; whites of two eggs, one pint of sweet cream; whip each seperately, then stir into soup. Serves eight persons.

OMELET FOR SIX.
Mrs. Eliza B. Smith.

Four eggs (whites and yellows beaten separately) salt to taste, mix all together, have griddle warm and greased, pour on your omelet, place in oven five or ten minutes to brown.

PARKER HOUSE ROLLS.
Mrs. Ella P. Hanna.

Boil one pint milk and cool it; take two quarts flour, two tablespoons lard, half cup white sugar, one cup yeast, a little salt. Beat well and let rise, then punch it; do the same again. Set about 9 a. m.; about 4 o'clock roll out about one-half inch thick and cut with biscuit cutter. Put three pieces of butter in each and fold together, pinching the edges.

POTATO SOUP.
Mrs. H. Warner.

Boil for three-fourths of an hour in just sufficient water to cover, four peeled potatoes, piece of celery, small piece of onion and whole mace.

Truth has a quiet breast.

At the same time boil three pints of milk, when potatoes are cooked mash, add butter, salt and a little pepper. Take milk from stove, strain potatoes through colander into milk, place on stove and boil up two or three times, then pour into tureen in which you have a little grated parsley and three tablespoons whipped cream.

DEVILED FISH.
Mrs. John E. Brewer.

One quart hot cream, two tablespoons butter, two heaping tablespoons corn starch, half teaspoon salt, half saltspoon white pepper, half teaspoon celery salt, a very little red pepper. Scald the cream, melt the butter in a quart sauce pan; when bubbling add the dry corn starch, stir until well mixed, add one-third of the cream, and stir as it boils and thickens, add more cream and boil again; when perfectly smooth add the rest of the cream; the sauce should be very thick; add the seasoning and mix while hot with fish. Bake in shells.

JELLY PIE.
Vie Harding.

Four eggs beaten seperately; one and half cups sugar, half cup butter, one cup milk, (half cream) one cup jelly, two tablespoons vanilla, one teaspoon flour or corn starch. Stir yolks of eggs, sugar and butter together, then add cream and jelly, (beaten fine) vanilla, and lastly the whites of eggs beaten to a froth. If a large cup is used this will make three pies.

BAKED HAM.

Soak for an hour in water, scrape and wipe; spread over a thin batter. Put in deep dish on sticks to keep out of gravy. Bake six or eight hours; remove skin and batter, sprinkle with two

Hodgens' for Fine Candies.

tablespoons sugar, black pepper and powdered crackers. Return to oven to brown. Stick in cloves and dust with cinnamon.

JELLIED VEAL.

Boil veal tender, pick up fine, put in mould with liquor it was boiled in; season well with pepper and salt. Press in a few hard boiled eggs.

VEAL SCOLLOP.
Mrs. W. S. Holliday.

Mince cold veal very fine; put a layer in the bottom of a buttered bake dish, season with pepper, salt and a little nutmeg. Put a layer of fine crumbs, next veal again and so on until full. Wet with good broth and put on top a layer of crumbs wet with milk and mixed with a beaten egg. If the oven is hot, cover with a pan and bake half an hour, then brown ten minutes.

DRESSING FOR COLD SLAW.
Mrs. W. S. Holliday.

Two eggs well beaten, two-thirds cup of vinegar, one teaspoon sugar, one heaping teaspoon of flour, small piece of butter, and a little mustard if desired; when these are beaten well together, boil and pour over slaw.

ORANGE SHORT CAKE.
Jennie Mitchell.

Three teaspoons baking powder to one quart of flour, add two tablespoons butter and thoroughly mix and add either milk or water to make a soft dough. Bake in two cakes, and when done split and spread with butter. For the filling remove the pulp from a half dozen oranges, sugar to taste. Drain off the juice and spread pulp between cakes. Serve with sauce. Sauce: One pint water, one tablespoon corn starch, two tablespoons butter, one cup sugar, and if preferred one well beaten egg; adding last the juice of oranges.

MINCE MEAT.
Mrs. Hugh Marshall.

Four pints chopped meat.
Four pints chopped suit.
Eight pints chopped apples.
One pint molasses, One quart of vinegar.
Three pounds of sugar.
Three tablespoons cinnamon.
One tablespoon of cloves.
Two tablespoons of mace. Two nutmegs.
Four lbs. raisins—two large and two seedless.
Salt and a little pepper. Citron and fruit juice is an improvement.

WHITE LAYER CAKE.
Mrs. Hugh Marshall.

Two cups sugar. Three cups flour.
Three-fourths cup butter. Three-fourths cup milk.
Whites eight eggs. Three teaspoons baking powder. Use any flavoring and filling desired.

FRENCH SALAD DRESSING.
Mrs. Melville Brewer.

Three tablespoons olive oil, one tablespoon vinegar, three saltspoons salt, one saltspoon black pepper. Serve on lettuce, mixed at table just before serving.

WASHING MADE EASY.
Mrs. Melville Brewer.

Eight ounces sal soda, six ounces borax, two and a half pounds Maple City Self-Washing soap, ten quarts rain water. Shave soap, add to water, with sal soda and borax. Heat until thoroughly dissolved—about an hour. Use half cup to each pail of water to soak clothes over night, add one cup to boil in. The mixture may be used only to boil the clothes, washing in usual way. It is excellent to whiten them and for washing flannels.

"Modest doubt is called the beacon of the wise."
—Troilus and Cressida.

FRAGMENTS.

"A good Wit will make use of anything." *Henry IV*.

A GOOD SUBSTITUTE FOR BUTTER, AND BEEF DRIPPINGS.

Get best kidney suet; put to boil in milk, allowing one-half teacup to each pound of suet; lift from bottom occasionally to prevent burning. When the milk has boiled out you can dip off grease, which will be of a delicate flavor. The suet is improved by soaking a few hours in cold water. Excellent to put with lard in frying doughnuts.

Pinch of salt helps the whites of eggs to beat more quickly.

Dough for breakfast rolls may be kept for several days on ice.

A spoonful of vinegar in a kettle of hot lard will prevent doughnuts from absorbing fat.

A few pieces of zinc put in a stove, where you use soft coal, will clean the pipe from soot.

Turpentine mixed with stove polish prevents rust and gives a higher gloss than water.

Mica in stoves can be made clean by washing with vinegar and water.

CLEANSING FLUID (Fine.)
Mrs. Geo. Wiley, Chicago.

Six drachms alcohol, two drachms ammonia, one drachm oil of sassafras, one drachm chloroform, $\frac{3}{4}$ drachm pulverized borax. Mix and shake well, then add one quart deodorized gasoline.

Few love to hear the sins they love to act.

Fresh lard will remove tar and grass stains.

Ink stains can be removed from the fingers by rubbing them with a match. The sulpher will soon erase all stains.

For washing clothes easily and securing best results in every way, the use of Maple City Self-Washing Soap is heartily recommended.

The best cement for mending china or glass is white lead. Put away three or four months before using.

Always keep mixed linseed oil and lime water in the house for burns Get the druggist to prepare 5 cents worth for you.

Apply hot water to a bruise. It will prevent swelling and discoloration.

Put two or three handsful of corn meal and one of graham flour in your buckwheat cakes.

5 cents worth of Chinese blue, dissolved in one quart of soft water and kept in corked bottles, makes an excellent bluing, and will last a family a year.

Eat oranges and cranberries for breakfast. They are good for the liver.

Give your children plenty of brown bread and milk, and well made corn meal bread, and fruit at meal times.

Try a teaspoon of kerosene in the water in which you wash windows and woodwork.

Use the white of an egg in making mustard plasters. If the mustard is strong, use part flour. This will prevent blistering.

Dissolve copperas in your drain pipes often to clean out the slime and grease and thoroughly disinfect them.

Better three hours too soon than a minute too late

For starching muslins dissolve one tablespoon of white gum arabic in a cup of water. Clean and dry your muslins before wetting in this solution. Iron right side down.

TO WASH BLANKETS.

One ounce pulverized borax, one-half pint soft soap. Put in cold soft water; soak over night. Rinse in two waters in morning, squeeze but not wring and hang up without wringing. For one blanket. Makes them soft and is easily done.

Pour sauce arouud puddings and fish, not over them.

Everything to be browned, should be handsomely browned, not burned.

Pineapple juice or grated pineapple added to lemonade is delicious.

Serve rich, creamy buttermilk with cracked ice. Healthful and nutritious.

One teaspoon sweet cream in frosting prevents crumbling when cut.

Pour hot water on raisins. They are more easily seeded.

To test eggs put them in water. If the large end turns up they are not fresh.

WEIGHTS AND MEASURES.

$2\frac{1}{2}$ Teaspoonfuls - - make One Tablespoonful
4 Tablespoonfuls - " One Wine-glassful
2 Wine-glassfuls - - " One Gill
2 Gills - - - " One Teacupful
2 Teacupfuls - - " One Pint
4 Teacupfuls Salt - - " One Ounce
$1\frac{1}{2}$ Tablespoonfuls Granulated
Sugar - - make One Ounce

Learning is but an adjunct to oneself.

2	Tablespoonfuls Flour	"	One Ounce
2	Cups or 1 Pint Granulated Sugar will weigh about		One Pound
1	Scant Quart Wheat Flour about		One Pound
10	Ordinary Sized Eggs	"	One Pound
	A piece of butter the size of an egg will weigh about		1½ Ounces
2	Cups of Butter -	"	One Pound
1	Quart Indian Meal	"	One Pound 4 oz
40	Drops -	"	One Teaspoonful
	A common sized Tumbler		One-half Pint
	A common sized Wine-glass		One-half Gill
2	Tablespoons Liquid make		One Ounce
1	Gill Liquid -	"	Four Ounces

TO SERVE ONE HUNDRED PERSONS.
Mrs. Eliza Smith.

Ham, 16 pounds; Chickens 6; Turkeys 2;. Oysters, 10 cans; Coffee, 2 pounds; Bread, 8 loaves; Saratoga Potatoes, 8 quarts; Layer Cakes 5; Angel Food 5; Ice Cream, 4 gallons; Fruit Salad, fill recipe 3 times.

"*Praise us as we are.tasted, allow us as we prov*
—*Troilus and Cressida.*

ESTABLISHED A QUARTER OF A CENTURY.

M. BREWER,

DRUGGIST

and dealers in

Wall Paper, Paints, Mouldings, Stationery, Glass, Etc. Picture Frames and Mats made on short notice and at very reasonable prices. Call and see for yourself.

Better is a Dinner of Herbs

On clean, fine linen than all the dainties of a palace served on an untidy table cloth. . . . .

We Sell Fine Linens

From Ireland, Scotland and Prussia. Cloths by the yard or pattern of any longth. Napkins of every size and quality. . . . .

Very Respectfully.

D. W. HARE & CO.

Square and Broadway,
MONMOUTH, ILL.

TRADE WITH

WARNER-JOEL CLOTHING CO.

57 S. SIDE SQUARE.

INDEX.

	PAGES.
Soup,	9– 16
Fish,	19– 23
Croquettes,	25– 28
Oysters,	30– 34
Meats,	36– 47
Vegetables,	49– 60
Salads,	62– 71
Cheese,	73– 75
Breads and Biscuits,	77– 85
Pies,	86– 96
Puddings and Sauces,	96–113
Ices,	114–120
Cakes,	121–145
Loaf Cake,	121–131
Layer Cakes,	131–139
Small Cakes,	139–145
Beverages,	147–151
Breakfast Dishes,	153–158
Eggs,	158–161
Pickles and Catsups,	161–169
Confectionery,	169–171
Addenda,	172–175
Fragments,	176–179
Weights and Measures,	178
Directory,	182–183

DIRECTORY.

"I had thought to have let in some of all professions."
—*Macbeth*.

Bates & Son, China Emporium, dealers in Groceries and Queensware.

Bosch & Co., Plumbers, Steam and Gas Fitters, 220 South First street.

W. W. Brooks, dealer in Staple and Fancy Groceries, near C., B. & Q. freight depot.

H. Burlingim, General Store, Fifth avenue and Third street.

Anna Cassel, Fine Millinery, South Main st.

O. M. Daymude, Dentist, Second National Bank building.

D. D. Diffenbaugh, Staple and Fancy Groceries, Fine Confections, Fruits, etc.

D. H. Evey, D. D. S., Office in People's National Bank Building.

O. F. Fowler, Meat Market, 205 E. Broadway.

G. N. Hawley. Dealer in Pianos and Organs, 111 North Main st., Monmouth, Ills.

W. S. Holliday, M. D., Physician and Surgeon, 208 South First st.

Hoy Brothers, Contractors and Builders, 513 South Third st.

Mrs. E. C. Johnson, Dealer in Stamping Patterns and Fancy Work Materials.

H. A. Johnson, Jewelry and Optical Goods. Eyes tested free. 105 East Broadway.

McNamara, Dealer in Staple and Fancy Groceries. 95 North Side Square.

Monmouth Gas Co. Gas Stoves at cost. Telephone 37.

Pollock Bros., Caterers and Confectioners, 107 East Broadway.

Red Star Cash Dry Goods Store, Dry Goods and Notions.

Peyton Roberts, Fire and Life Insurance, Main street and Square.

Republican Printing Co.

H. W. Sisson, Manufacturer of Harness Specialties and Horse Clothing, 107 North Main st.

W. R. Skinner, I. C. Meat Market.

W. P. Smith, Dentist, Over Second National Bank, Monmouth, Ills.

Tred. H. Smith, Watchmaker and Engraver. Rooms over Second National Bank.

J. W. Spriggs & Co., Boots and Shoes, 106 South Main street.

Spriggs & Son, Druggists.

J. D. Suggs, Dealer in Staple and Fancy Groceries, opposite Iowa Central Depot.

J. Sullivan & Co., Hardware, Farm Machinery and Plumbing.

W. T. Steffen, Cash Meat Market, 708 South First street.

Drs. Taylor & Ebersole, Homeopathists, Monmouth National Bank Building.

John N. Thomson, "The Fair."

Dr. A. J. Waid, Dentist. Teeth extracted without pain and ulcerated teeth saved.

R. E. White, Undertaker, S. E. Corner Square.

Woods & Son, Boots and Shoes, North Side Square.

Blackburn & Turnbull,
UNDERTAKERS.

Leading Liverymen, 'Bus and Carriage Line.

Office open day and night. Calls answered at all hours.

Special attention to Carriage work for Parties, Weddings, et.

316 to 322 South Main Street.

DON'T FORGET THE MONMOUTH **Lumber Co.** —FOR— **Ladd Coal,** When You Are A Cooking.

WEST BROADWAY

YOU CAN'T do good cooking without GOOD FUEL

THE LADD COAL beats everything.

Try It!

WEST BROADWAY

T BROADWAY.

www.ingramcontent.com/pod-product-compliance
Lightning Source LLC
Chambersburg PA
CBHW032152160426
43197CB00008B/875